JOAN FITZPATRICK DEAN

TOM STOPPARD

COMEDY AS A MORAL MATRIX

A LITERARY FRONTIERS EDITION

UNIVERSITY OF MISSOURI PRESS

COLUMBIA & LONDON, 1981

Library of Congress Cataloging in Publication Data

Dean, Joan F. 1949–
    Tom Stoppard: Comedy as a Moral Matrix.

    (A Literary frontiers edition)
    1. Stoppard, Tom—Criticism and interpretation.
I. Title.
PR6069.T6Z63   822'.914   80-26400
ISBN 0-8262-0332-9

All passages from Tom Stoppard's works are reprinted by permission of Grove Press.

FOR MY PARENTS

Acknowledgments

I am grateful to the Research Council at the University of Missouri at Kansas City for its support and to my colleagues, Maxine Moore and Robert L. Dean, for their careful readings. Stephen Gosnell and Louis Cicotello were generous and helpful in discussing the works of Magritte and other artists. Albert E. Kalson offered a perceptive and knowledgeable commentary for which I am indeed grateful. I also want to thank S. P. S., and I am, as always, deeply indebted to J. R. C.

TOM STOPPARD

I

Since *Rosencrantz and Guildenstern Are Dead* was first presented by Britain's National Theatre in 1967, Tom Stoppard has emerged as a major dramatist whose plays have generated enormous commercial success while confounding critics. His three most important works to date, *Rosencrantz and Guildenstern*, *Jumpers* (1972), and *Travesties* (1974), have been produced both in the West End and on Broadway. In 1977, Kenneth Ewing, Stoppard's agent, estimated that *Rosencrantz and Guildenstern* had "'grossed well over three hundred thousand pounds.'"[1] Stoppard's works have been widely produced by the regional theatrical companies in both Great Britain and the United States.

In 1967, Stoppard won the John Whiting Award and an *Evening Standard* Award for *Rosencrantz and Guildenstern*; the following year he was honored with the Prix Italia for *Albert's Bridge,* an hour-long radio play. He has won the Tony Award, the New York Critics Circle Award, and the Shakespeare Award. Kenneth Tynan identifies Stoppard as "one of the two or three most prosperous and ubiquitously adulated playwrights at present bearing a British passport" (p. 46). Although there is consensus among the critics about Stoppard's masterful control of language and plot, many commentators assert that his plays do not withstand rigorous philosophical scrutiny. In this regard, John Gardner's comments in *On Moral Fiction* are typical:

> The plays have no conclusions, and in fact from the outset the existential accidents on which the thought of the plays depends are so obviously contrived, like the too-easily manipulated elements of a farce, that we're discouraged from expecting more than a theatrical finale. . . . But the tone, the ultra-threatrical pizzazz, the delightfully flashy language which is Stoppard's special gift—all these warn us in advance that the treatment of ideas is likely to be more fashionable than earnest-predictable talk about the meaninglessness of things, the impossibility of "knowing," and so on.[2]

1. Kenneth Tynan, *Show People* (New York: Simon and Schuster, 1979), p. 49.
2. John Gardner, *On Moral Fiction* (New York: Basic Books, 1978), pp. 58–59.

Gardner puritanically implies that Stoppard's theatricalism, farce, and verbal wit are incompatible with or at least inappropriate to great (and as he sees it moral) art. A similar sentiment is voiced by John Russell Taylor, who, couching his criticism in the vagaries of cant, fails to venture the specifics of his charges:

> Perhaps the doubts I feel to some extent about all Stoppard's work boil down, rather surprisingly, to a feeling that he lacks a sort of fundamental seriousness as a playwright, that his ideas remain, in the Coleridgean definition, on the level of fancy rather than imagination.[3]

What Coleridge called fancy, the mechanical, aggregative power that receives its material from association, is clearly the starting point of Stoppard's talents and the characteristic of his works universally acclaimed. Julius Novick, writing in *The Village Voice*, is inclined to see this faculty almost as an end in itself, calling Stoppard "the most brilliantly playful of living playwrights," but also adding:

> As for *Travesties*, I have maintained that there is something serious in Mr. Stoppard's *refusal* to be serious about the serious matters he deals with in that play: a paradox that Wilde would have found congenial. In *Travesties*, as in so much of Wilde's own work, playfulness becomes a kind of assertion of freedom.[4]

Travesties elicited a comparable, although less favorable, opinion from Gerald Weales:

> Stoppard has been doing a soft-shoe around existential chaos ever since he turned up in the English theatre, and *Travesties* is either his blackest statement to date or his assumption that the surface joke is what counts.[5]

3. John Russell Taylor, *The Second Wave: British Drama for the Seventies* (New York: Hill and Wang, 1971), p. 107.

4. Julius Novick, "Going Plume on Plume," *The Village Voice* (31 January 1977), p. 69.

5. Gerald Weales, "The Stage," review of *Travesties, Commonweal* (13 February 1976) p. 114.

In short, Stoppard has dazzled his audiences and critics with dramatic pyrotechnics, delighted them with verbal acrobatics, and teased them with philosophical speculation; but like his two strippers, the secretary in *Jumpers* and Cecily in *Travesties*, he has left some of his audience frustrated.

When *Rosencrantz and Guildenstern* first appeared, some critics attempted to identify Stoppard as an existentialist. Irving Wardle wrote that Stoppard "manages to provide his two heroes with an existential development."[6] In 1967, Stoppard himself said he was interested in Rosencrantz and Guildenstern "as existential immortals,"[7] but by 1974 he would refute that:

> First I must say that I didn't know what the word "existential" meant until it was applied to *Rosencrantz*. And even now existentialism is not a philosophy I find either attractive or plausible.[8]

The debate over the philosophical validity of Stoppard's work in general and *Jumpers* in particular even found its way into scholarly circles, not just among academia's literary critics, but also among its philosophers. Sir Alfred J. Ayer, Wykeham Professor of Logic at Oxford University, wrote that he "enormously enjoyed Tom Stoppard's *Jumpers*... and came away feeling the greatest respect for its author."[9] In 1975, the editors of the prestigious British journal *Philosophy* devoted fourteen pages to Jonathan Bennett's attack on Stoppard. The next year, the same editors printed a rebuttal to Bennett's argument.

It appears both ironic and unfair that charges of philosophical obscurity and evasiveness are so often leveled against Stoppard but rarely against other playwrights—Harold Pinter, for instance. In no small part

---

6. Irving Wardle quoted in "Tom Stoppard Interviewed by Giles Gordon," *Transatlantic Review* 29 (1968): 17.

7. Tom Stoppard, "The Definite Maybe," *Author* 78 (1967): 19.

8. Stoppard, "Ambushes for the Audience," *Theatre Quarterly* 4 (1974): 6.

9. Alfred J. Ayer, "Love Among the Logical Positivists," *Sunday (London) Times* (9 April 1972), p. 16.

this criticism of Stoppard is due to the fact that he usually relies upon the logically structured plot suggested by the well-made play or farce. Governed by causality, many of his plays appear naturalistic or realistic in dramaturgy despite his manipulation of the fourth wall. But once the logical premises of his works are established, Stoppard pursues those premises to their inexorable and sometimes illogical conclusions. From absurdism and expressionism, certainties and resolutions are not demanded; without their initial grounding in logic and with their attendant assumption of uncertainty if not meaninglessness, absurdism and expressionism do not offer clear-cut, well-defined solutions. But then neither does Stoppard.

Stoppard's dependence on logic is nearly as flawless as it is pervasive. The Coda to *Jumpers*, presented as the protagonist's nightmare, is a notable exception, but even in it the reiteration of a structural pattern makes it intelligible. In Stoppard's plays, logic is the admittedly delicate and sometimes superficial linchpin that holds society as well as the plays themselves together; remove it and all collapses. The peculiar internal logic of his works is not always easily transferred to the world outside the plays. But within them, logic, however manipulated, distorted, or contorted, is the organizational principal that guarantees their comic success.

Stoppard himself has repeatedly insisted that he does not intend to produce any systematic or even coherent vision:

> The element which I find most valuable is the one that other people are put off by—that is, that there is very often *no* single, clear statement in my plays. What there is, is a series of conflicting statements made by conflicting characters, and they tend to play a sort of infinite leap-frog. You know, an argument, a refutation, then a rebuttal of the refutation, then a counter-rebuttal, so that there is never any point in this intellectual leap-frog at which I feel *that* is the speech to stop it on, that is the last word.
>
> ("Ambushes," pp. 6–7)

Furthermore, Stoppard suggests that didactic art is not simply a subject matter:

There are political plays... which are about specific situations, and there are political plays which are about a general political situation, and there are plays which are *political* acts in themselves, insofar as it can be said that attacking or insulting or shocking an audience is a political act (and it *is* said). There are also plays *about* politics which are about as political as *Charley's Aunt*. ... *Jumpers* reflects my belief that all political acts have a moral basis to them and are meaningless without it. *Travesties* asks whether the words "revolutionary" and "artist" are capable of being synonymous, or whether they are mutually exclusive or something in between.

I'm not impressed by art *because* it's political. I believe in art being good art or bad art, not relevant or irrelevant art. The plain truth is that if you are angered or disgusted by a particular injustice or immorality, and you want to do something about it, *now*, at once, then you can hardly do worse than write a play about it. That's what art is bad at.[10]

When Stoppard deals with injustice or immorality or even with philosophical questions, he does so not with splenetic or didactic wrath; rather he considers these questions with an objectivity that produces the high theatrics and witty dialogue which are his trademarks.

Among literary and dramatic critics, scholarship on Stoppard comes primarily from three sources: Kenneth Tynan, C. W. E. Bigsby, and Ronald Hayman. Tynan's piece, which first appeared as an essay in his series of profiles for *The New Yorker* and has since been published in *Show People*, draws upon his personal acquaintance with Stoppard. It is probably the most sensible, sensitive consideration of Stoppard that is currently available. Not only is it filled with intriguing anecdotes about Stoppard's guarded private life but it also contains valuable information on the original productions of *Rosencrantz and Guildenstern*, *Jumpers*, and *Travesties*. During the late sixties and early seventies, Tynan was the literary manager of Britain's National Theatre, which mounted the first London produc-

10. Stoppard quoted in Charles Marowitz, "Tom Stoppard—The Theatre's Intellectual P. T. Barnum," *The New York Times* (19 October 1975), sec. 2, p. 5.

tion of both *Rosencrantz and Guildenstern* and *Jumpers*. But Tynan's essay is most significant because it is the first clear articulation of Stoppard's own views on the themes of his plays. Bigsby's pamphlet for the British Council was published in 1976; it deals mainly with the three full-length works Stoppard had produced for the commercial stage by that date. Bigsby is particularly adept at identifying the varied and complex influences—from Wittgenstein to Wilde to Beckett—that appear in Stoppard's work. Hayman's book is a play-by-play study that relies heavily upon the author's unabashed enthusiasm for Stoppard and the synopses of each work up to 1977. It contains two valuable interviews with Stoppard (both held in 1976) as well as the only information published in the United States on several of Stoppard's minor works.

Throughout his career, Stoppard evinces a penchant for parody of popular dramatic genres, such as the whodunnit, the historical or parahistorical play, or musical comedy. His strong parodic impulse is at least indirectly responsible for both the commercial success and the critical attacks of Stoppard. The whodunnit, for instance, with its clichés of suspense and intrigue, is the starting point for *The Real Inspector Hound* (1968), *Jumpers,* and *Artist Descending a Staircase* (1972). In each instance, a murder triggers the highly convoluted, even frenzied activity that serves as a plot. In *Jumpers,* the question of who murdered McFee is never answered definitively; in *Hound,* the murdered man proves to be the victim of mistaken identity. The suspense generated by the murder inevitably is a red herring that diverts, while entertaining, the audience.

Stoppard's inclination toward parody grows out of his experience as a drama critic in Bristol and London. At the age of seventeen, he secured a job at the *Bristol Evening World* and later at the *Western Daily Press.* In the late fifties, Bristol, a city of about 250,000 people, was theatrically active with a number of companies (both professional and amateur) presenting conventional adaptations from Agatha Christie's fiction, classics from the Elizabethan and Jacobean stages, and an inordinately large number of plays by Oscar Wilde. Indeed, at one point in the spring of 1958 there were four simultaneous offerings or adaptations of

Wilde's *The Importance of Being Earnest*.[11] By 1960, Stoppard was the regular film reviewer for the *Bristol Evening World*. One of his lengthiest columns of that year was a comparison of two films based on Wilde's life (which appeared simultaneously in Bristol): *Oscar Wilde* and *The Trials of Oscar Wilde*. In this 1960 article, whose title "The Importance of Being Oscar: Two Studios Hear the Call of the Wilde" could only have come from Stoppard, he identifies himself "as a confirmed addict and admirer (literary) of Wilde."[12] At the time, Stoppard was twenty-one years old.

It is difficult to overestimate Wilde's influence on Stoppard. The most obvious evidence of Stoppard's debt to Wilde is found in *Travesties*, where the plot of *The Importance of Being Earnest* is superimposed on the love interests between Tristan Tzara and Gwendolen Carr and between Henry Carr and Cecily. Tzara blends with Wilde's character Jack Worthing; Carr merges with Wilde's Algernon Moncrieff; James Joyce plays the role suggested by Lady Bracknell; Gwendolen and Cecily retain the names used by Wilde. Beyond the debt indicated by *Travesties*, Tynan points out that the germ of the idea for *Rosencrantz and Guildenstern* might well have come from Wilde's opinion of Shakespeare's courtiers:

> I know of nothing in all Drama more incomparable from the point of view of Art, or more suggestive in its subtlety of observation, than Shakespeare's drawing of Rosencrantz and Guildenstern. They are Hamlet's college friends. They have been his companions.... At the moment when they come across him in the play he is staggering under the weight of a burden intolerable to one of his temperament.... Of all this, Guildenstern and Rosencrantz realise nothing.[13]

Whereas these instances bespeak his specific borrowings from Wilde, Stoppard's intricate wordplay, witty repartee,

11. Peter Rodford, "On Plays and People," *Western Daily Press* (14 April 1958), p. 4.

12. "The Importance of Being Oscar: Two Studies Hear the Call of the Wilde," *Bristol Evening World* (29 April 1960), p. 3.

13. Oscar Wilde, *De Profundis* (New York: Avon, 1964), p. 176. Quoted by Tynan, in *Show People*, pp. 84–85.

and tour de force conclusions suggest the breadth of Wilde's influence.

Wilde's views of art—its functions, responsibilities, and nature—are sometimes taken up by Stoppard to check his impulse toward overtly substantive statements. Wilde's art for art's sake aesthetic often counterbalances Stoppard's social or political commentary, especially in his more recent works.

Stoppard continued his career as a drama critic in London where he reviewed for *Scene* magazine between December 1962 and April 1963. During that time, he saw 132 plays, the reviews of which often bore the pseudonym William Boot. (Tynan, p. 66). His career as a critic ended abruptly when *Scene* ceased publication on 20 April 1963. All of this playgoing, however, left him with a remarkably keen appreciation of the formulas of drama as well as its theatricalism. Over the next twelve years, the derivative quality of his work, particularly its formulaic and theatrical elements, sometimes threatened to overtake his thematic interests.

Stoppard's decision to become a playwright is ascribed to several motives. In 1967 he stated that "in July 1960 . . . I remembered that it was my twenty-third birthday; twenty-three and still unpublished, unstaged . . ." ("Definite Maybe," p. 18). Later he attributed his decision to "historical accident. After 1956 everybody of my age wanted to write plays" ("Ambushes," p. 4). The year 1956 was, of course, the pivotal year for postwar British drama—the year of John Osborne's *Look Back in Anger*; the year of the angry young men; the year of the English Stage Company's first season at the Royal Court Theatre. Tynan is more specific in identifying Stoppard's inspiration:

> In reality, it was [Peter] O'Toole's blazing performances— and the plays they adorned in Bristol [*Hamlet* and *Look Back in Anger*] that turned Stoppard on to theatre. By the end of the [1957–58] season, he was incubating a new vocation.
> (Tynan, p. 59)

At the moment of the flowering of postwar theatre in Britain, Stoppard's experience as a reviewer, his attraction to the glamour and sophistication of the theatre, and his fascination with language all pointed to a career of play-writing.

The first level of Stoppard's work—that of sheer entertainment—is the most obvious demonstration of the lessons he learned as a reviewer. Some critics have viewed his plays as farce and, in turn, have seen his characters as the caricatures inherent to that dramatic genre. Jill Levenson comments that "Stoppard's characters are rarely three dimensional";[14] Gabriele Scott Robinson asserts that his characters "are personifications of ideas, always subordinate to a conceit."[15] Part of the critical frustration with his characters lies in the fact that his plays are usually populated either by famous people or famous characters from other plays; these characters, however, never conform to the expectations of the audience. Stoppard, in fact, depends upon the betrayal of stereotypes to breathe new life into the characters he re-creates. These astounding and often ludicrous characterizations are typical of his technique and indicative of his commitment to ambushing his audiences.

Characterization for Stoppard, however, is preceded by his selection of subject; once he has chosen the subject of his plays, the characters emerge logically. As he said in 1979:

> I don't respond to the real situation outside my windows; that isn't really what inspires me to write. You see, I'm really not very good on character. My plays . . . are entirely plays of ideas; which is to say I am interested in a particular debate and thereafter I'm in a desperate search for some people who will speak in this debate. Furthermore, they all have to speak like me, regardless. If I need an African president and I need him to enter a debate about British journalism, then I just have to make sure my African president was educated at an English public school.[16]

14. Jill Levenson, "Views from a Revolving Door: Stoppard's Canon to Date," *Queen's Quarterly* 58 (1971): 431.

15. Gabriele Scott Robinson, "Plays without Plots: The Theatre of Tom Stoppard," *Educational Theatre Journal* 29 (1977): 38.

16. Stoppard, National Press Club luncheon (11 October 1979), Washington, D.C.

Hence, Stoppard borrows characters from other dramatic works (for example, *Hamlet, Macbeth, The Importance of Being Earnest*), discovers them in history (V. I. Lenin, Henry Carr, James Joyce), parodies the stereotypes of well-established genres (as in the succession of police inspectors and detectives taken from the whodunnit), or models them loosely on contemporary individuals (Vladimir Bukovsky, Pavel Kohout, and possibly Alfred J. Ayer). His characters may serve as mouthpieces for specific ideologies, but none speaks with Stoppard's own voice. His real talent in characterization lies in restraining himself from idealizing those characters with whom he sympathizes and from undermining those with whom he does not.

Perhaps because his plays do not rely upon conventionally realized or original characters, his protagonists—whether philosophy professors, drama critics, or diplomatic factotums—often are cut from the same cloth. Typically, they are loners who stand on the fringe of some momentous action. They are often sincere eccentrics desperately trying to reassert their faith in themselves or in humanity in spite of their familiarity with failure and unhappiness. Rosencrantz and Guildenstern are not the first of Stoppard's characters to embody these traits; even George Riley, the protagonist of *Enter a Free Man* (1968) [and its adaptation, *A Walk on the Water* (1963)], illustrates them. George has such a sincere belief in himself (as well as the entire system of free enterprise) that he can believe that reusable envelopes are marketable and that he is lovable. Stoppard suggests this optimistic streak in referring to George's "tattered dignity."[17] Similarly, Rosencrantz's and Guildenstern's summons to Elsinore and commission to "glean what afflicts" Hamlet are not undertaken without optimism. They earnestly attempt to behave responsibly, however shallow their moral convictions, and to do their level best in a situation that they cannot hope to understand.

In Stoppard's most important works of the seventies, *Jumpers* and *Travesties*, the character type is again witness-

17. C. W. E. Bigsby, *Tom Stoppard: Writers and Their Works*, No. 273 (London: Longmans for the British Council, 1976), p. 8.

ed in George Moore and Henry Carr. Both Moore and Carr struggle to understand and to justify their lives, their proximity to greatness, and their claims to immortality, but, like Rosencrantz and Guildenstern, they hardly comprehend the world they inhabit. Neither Moore nor Carr is qualified to offer an accurate account of himself; nonetheless, both attempt to rationalize their convictions through either philosophical lectures (in Moore's case) or memoirs (in Carr's case). Stoppard's technique in presenting Moore's lecture and Carr's memoirs is essentially identical: each steps outside the dramatic action in a monologue but pursues wild tangents rather than his original points; repeatedly he must stop himself and start over again. The chaos at Moore's fashionable apartment—featuring a stripping secretary swinging on a trapeze, a neurotic wife in the throes of nervous collapse, a murdered colleague suspended from a bedroom door—constantly interrupts the composition of his lecture. Carr's dictation of his memoirs is likewise interrupted by the historical realities of Zurich in 1918; moreover, his memory occasionally runs amok. If only because Carr knew or at least knew of so many famous people and Moore knows or at least is employed to debate his ability to know, each has a fervent desire to show that his life has not been wasted.

In *Night and Day* (1978) Stoppard's character type does not precisely follow the pattern established in the earlier works for two reasons: first, the play's protagonist is a woman, Ruth Carson; second, its dramaturgy is much more straightforward than that of *Jumpers* or *Travesties*. Like Rosencrantz and Guildenstern, Ruth finds herself standing in the wings of momentous action. While her husband and a trio of British reporters are involved in political revolution, she plays hostess and mistress. And like Moore and Carr, Ruth has a dramatic outlet for her own thoughts, not in the composition of a lecture or her memoirs, but through "Ruth"—the ironic, self-critical inner voice whose asides and soliloquies are not heard by the other characters on stage.

This basic line of development of Stoppard's recurrent character type not only appears in his full-length works but also pervades his radio dramas, short stories, television scripts, and other creative works. Even the names of his characters—from George Riley to George Moore and from Carr to Ruth Carson—echo one another. Often his use of the same name for ostensibly dissimilar characters suggests their mutual affinities. The most celebrated example of Stoppard's recurrent names are the Moons of *Lord Malquist and Mr. Moon* and *The Real Inspector Hound* and the Boots of "The Dissolution of Dominic Boot" and *The Real Inspector Hound* (in which the character is actually named Birdboot.) The Georges of his plays (Riley from *Enter a Free Man* and Moore from *Jumpers*) also have more in common than a cursory glance might suggest. Both boast of success and ambition but both are overshadowed by the women in their lives: Persephone efficiently manages their household; Moore's wife, Dorothy, not only provides the income to support a lavish London address but also is responsible for his introduction to Bertrand Russell. Bigsby's comment on Moore, "all of George's convictions seem to be invalidated by events" (p. 20), is equally applicable to Riley and his inventions.

Even in his earliest works Stoppard gravitates toward protagonists who are on the periphery of importance, sometimes on the periphery of life itself. But the evolution of Stoppard's work is not confined to the development of a character type; it can also be seen in the recurrence of certain themes. Often these themes, such as the importance of perspective and the relativity of perception, are subsidiary to the main focus of the plot, but they are particularly well suited to the recurrent character type.

Stoppard's plays also illustrate his attraction to self-contained systems that initially depend on a priori assumptions, but thereafter proceed with exacting logic. The study of philosophy, the structure of farce, and the microcosm of the whodunnit are three examples of such self-contained systems. All are like games in their adherence to strict rules. Stoppard's comment on his attraction toward philosophy, "I enjoyed the rules that philosophers play by,"[18] confirms this. Moreover, the settings of his plays frequently reflect his propensity toward self-contained systems. In the early plays, his characters often seek refuge

18. Ronald Hayman, *Tom Stoppard* (Totowa, N.J.: Rowman and Littlefield, 1977), p. 1.

from the world—in a convent, a hospital, or a bar, for instance. Later, in *Jumpers, Travesties,* and *Night and Day,* characters are at least ostensibly secluded from the upheaval of the world—in the Moores' apartment, in Zurich during World War I, in the Carsons' African home. But the political realities in these later plays intrude into the security and isolation of these settings. His most recent plays, set in Russian asylums or Eastern European countries, confront political realities much more directly.

Stoppard's increasing willingness to address political questions is the most important characteristic of his evolution as a dramatist. His earliest plays, written in the early and mid-sixties, are an apprenticeship in which he dispenses with the impulse toward naturalistic dramaturgy, establishes himself as a minor playwright, and explores the nature of the various media (radio, television, and fiction, in addition to stage drama). With the success of *Rosencrantz and Guildenstern* in 1967, Stoppard secures a foothold in the dramatic world that frees him to develop what will emerge as his eclectic but distinctive style. The plays of the late sixties continue to pursue the potential inherent to radio and television in works like *If You're Glad I'll Be Frank* (1966) and *Albert's Bridge* (1968). This same period also sees the production of *The Real Inspector Hound* and *After Magritte,* two short plays that solidify Stoppard's reputation as a parodist and master craftsman of plot. With *Jumpers, Artist Descending a Staircase,* and *Travesties,* he enters a new phase in his playwrighting—one that witnesses the emergence of his specific concern with art, philosophy, and morality. These three works, two stage plays and one radio drama, fulfill the promise suggested by his early works but also anticipate the waning of his theatrical high jinks and the waxing of his involvement in political matters in his subsequent plays. Stoppard's most recent plays, that is, his plays since *Travesties,* evince a preoccupation with social and political issues, yet *Every Good Boy Deserves Favor* (1977), *Professional Foul* (1977), *Night and Day,* and even *Cahoot's Macbeth* (1979) are certainly not turgid polemics. They, in fact, treat politics in much the same way that *Jumpers* treats philosophy.

The most striking characteristic of Stoppard's work is his unremitting self-consciousness. On the first level, this introspective quality manifests itself in his deliberate mining of theatrical resources. Along with other postwar dramatists, he has reclaimed and revamped the vehicles for direct address to the audience, notably the music-hall chairman and the Renaissance soliloquy, which violate the fourth wall of representational dramaturgy. Stoppard's experience as a reviewer taught him not only the formulas of drama but also what works well on stage. His borrowings from Wilde and Shakespeare, as well as his parodies, are indicative of his consciousness of writing in a dramatic tradition.

On the second level, this self-consciousness gives rise to the play metaphor that draws the analogy between all men and actors and between life and the stage. In *Rosencrantz and Guildenstern*, the play metaphor is implicit in the relationship between the title characters and the Tragedians; in *The Real Inspector Hound*, it appears when the drama critics change places with the actors.

Third, Stoppard's self-consciousness directs him to question the artist, his responsibilities, and his place in society. In *Artist Descending a Staircase* and *Travesties*, he provides a forum for representatives of various aesthetic theories to voice their opinions. In *Night and Day*, journalists rather than artists must face the question of their responsibility to society.

Finally, the self-consciousness of Tom Stoppard leads him to challenge the validity and meaning of art. Underlying Stoppard's self-consciousness is a self-criticism that takes as its point of departure Auden's statement that art never saved anyone from death in a concentration camp, a comment Stoppard is fond of quoting. Stoppard's carefully cultivated refusal to moralize in his early works later yields at least to a concern with specific political issues, yet he never envisions a political purpose to his art. His aim, surprisingly, is much higher—toward morality not just politics. Stoppard is quoted as saying that "when, because, art takes notice of something important, it's claimed that the art is important. It's not" ("Ambushes," p. 14); rather, the issue that art notices, he implies, retains its importance. Elsewhere, Stoppard indicates that art itself is indeed important not merely as entertainment or spectacle, but because "it provides the moral matrix, the moral sensibility, from which we make our judgments about the world" ("Ambushes," p. 17). From his apprenticeship in naturalistic dramaturgy through his reconsideration of the themes as well as characters of *Hamlet* to his concentration on particular political injustices, Stoppard's plays do indeed suggest such a moral matrix with increasing clarity and insight.

II

Before *Rosencrantz and Guildenstern* appeared in London, Stoppard composed nearly a dozen published or performed works. Several of these early works remain unpublished: *The Gamblers* (1965), *The Dissolution of Dominic Boot* (1964), and two television plays, *Teeth* and *Another Moon Called Earth* (both 1967). Others, such as *A Walk on the Water*, were adapted for one medium from another. Still others are not plays at all, but excursions into the realm of fiction.

The three short stories published in *Introduction: Stories by New Writers* (1964) are unlike anything else that Stoppard has written inasmuch as they are largely autobiographical. "Life, Times: Fragments," for instance, concerns a young journalist who hears time's winged chariot thundering down upon him. The episodic story follows the trail of rejection slips left by this man over the course of thirty years. In light of the denial of earthly rewards, the protagonist grows closer to God. He abandons his career as a writer to pursue the Lord and reconciles himself to acceptance by the Almighty as compensation for a lifetime of rejection. The sad truth that confronts him at the end of the story is characteristic of the ironic tone heard in many of Stoppard's plays: " 'The Lord thanks you for your contribution but regrets that it is not quite suitable for the Kingdom of Heaven.' "[1] "Life, Times: Fragments" is laced with lines that resurface in Stoppard's work. As the writer muses over his wasted life he says:

> Do not despair: one of the thieves was saved.
> Do not presume: one of the thieves was damned.
> Very nice, that. St. Augustine, I believe.

> (p. 129)

The lines can be found in *Rosencrantz and Guildenstern* as well as *Waiting for Godot*; the common source, however, is indeed Augustine. Later the writer will say, "I am drowning with the panache of someone walking on the water"

---

1. Stoppard, "Life, Times: Fragments," *Introduction* (London: Faber, 1964), p. 129.

(p. 129)—a phrase that reappears as the title of the television adaptation of *Enter a Free Man*—*A Walk on the Water*.

"Reunion" is an uncharacteristically emotionally charged work in which a man and a woman, "old friends" (p. 121), see each other after the woman's husband has abandoned her. It is a surprisingly romantic story focused on an ineffable, undefinable "faith," a faith that would drive a person to murder or to shout an obscenity in a place dedicated to silence. Like many of Stoppard's purists and believers, this man's faith is stymied by insensitivity; the woman shuts out his faith first by flippantly agreeing with him and finally by telling him to shut up.

The last of his three short stories, "The Story," is interesting in light of *Night and Day*; both draw heavily upon Stoppard's experience as a newspaperman; both illustrate the enormous and often abused power of the press. In both "The Story" and *Night and Day*, a journalist sets out to get his story only to satisfy an editor and to advance his career. But in each instance the reporter's lack of honor and conscience precipitates a needless death.

Two years after these short stories were published, Stoppard's only novel, *Lord Malquist and Mr. Moon* (1966), appeared. It received little critical attention and even less commercial success. Its protagonist, Moon, sees himself as the twentieth-century's answer to the eighteenth century's Boswell. He stumbles upon Lord Malquist, who is just as ill at ease with this century as is Moon and who hires Moon to write his journals. The novel begins as several different groups are converging on Picadilly Circus on the day of Winston Churchill's funeral. Moon, Malquist, and their driver (a black Irishman named O'Hara) travel in a baroque pink coach befitting their eighteenth-century pretensions. Another group consists of two men dressed as cowboys to advertise Western Trails Pork and Beans. (Eventually, these two, Long John Slaughter and Jasper Jones, will stage a shoot out at Traflagar Square in their quest to attain Jane, Moon's wife.) Third is Jane and Marie, her French maid. Fourth is Lady Malquist and her lion, Rollo. Finally, there is "the Risen Christ," an itinerant on muleback who insists that all he needs to save the world is the attention of the multitude.

Moon is principally interesting for the characteristics

he shares with Stoppard's other protagonists, especially George Moore in *Jumpers,* and for his name. Like George, Moon is at work on a magnum opus that he will, in all likelihood, never complete. Moon's project is even more ambitious than George's philosophical work in progress; Moon plans to publish a history of the world. Moon is also like George in that both their wives are openly unfaithful to them. But even more important is the common temperament of George and Moon—that temperament allies both of them with a succession of characters named Moon (and Boot) who appear in Stoppard's work.

The recurrence of Moons and Boots in Stoppard's work is primarily confined to his early works: "The Dissolution of Dominic Boot," *Lord Malquist and Mr. Moon, The Real Inspector Hound,* and Stoppard's own use of Boot as a journalistic pseudonym. The name *Moon* derives from an idiosyncratic association with a scene in *Left-Handed Gun; Boot* from the character by that name in Evelyn Waugh's *Scoop.* Stoppard's Boots often are more ostentatious and outgoing, often in fact more dominant than the submissive Moons. Stoppard himself describes a Moon as "a person to whom things happen. Boot is rather more aggressive" (Tynan, p. 67). Although Stoppard's characters frequently come in pairs (such as Lord Malquist and Mr. Moon, Birdboot and Moon, George Moore and Archibald Jumper, Rosencrantz and Guildenstern), they rarely appear with a clear dominant personality and an obviously submissive one. Instead, one often appears more methodical, systematic, and ambitious while the other, caught in a quagmire of indecision, comes to depend on his partner.

The Moon character, reflecting another's light rather than emitting his own, is also related to the moon imagery that appears throughout Stoppard's work. He has said that:

> Years and years ago, before a moon-landing seemed imminent at all, I thought, I *felt,* that the destruction of moon mythology and moon association in poetry and romance, superstition and everything, would be a sort of minute lobotomy performed on the human race, like a tiny laser making dead some small part of the psyche.
>
> ("Ambushes," p. 17)

He may well have had in mind Shakespeare's lines from *A Midsummer Night's Dream*: "The lunatic, the lover, and the poet are of imagination all compact..." (5.1.7–8). Although many of Stoppard's early works are unpublished or seldom produced, they are important and interesting as precursors for his later, more successful plays. Three— " 'M' is for Moon Among Other Things" (1964), *Enter a Free Man* (1968), and "A Separate Peace" (1966), each written for a different medium—foreshadow the themes and dramaturgy that will characterize Stoppard's mature plays.

" 'M' is for Moon Among Other Things," a fifteen-minute radio play broadcast in 1964 by the BBC's Radio Four, is less important for its own merits than for the similarities it shares with the later plays. Here Stoppard employs two of his favorite techniques that will reappear frequently over the next ten years and that will culminate in *Travesties*. The first is a structural device that juxtaposes a domestic or otherwise personal situation with a historical event that receives worldwide attention; the second, a technique that enables the audience to know a character's thoughts.

Constance and Alfred, the childless couple who are the only characters in " 'M' is for Moon," lead a life so humdrum and banal that the arrival of the latest installment of a mail-order encyclopedia, the evening news report, or a quarrel over dinner arrangements are its highlights. A particular (and typical) evening finds Constance reading through her newly arrived M-to-N volume while Alfred peruses the newspaper. The historical event that counterpoints their lives is announced in the evening news: Marilyn Monroe has been found dead. As Alfred contemplates her plight ("It's such a cold shallow world she was living in. No warmth or understanding—no one understood her, she was friendless."),[2] he constructs a fantasy in which he counsels and consoles Monroe. Ironically, he remains oblivious of his wife's analogous circumstance; Constance, too, lives in a world devoid of warmth and understanding.

Monroe's death, like Churchill's funeral in *Lord Malquist and Mr. Moon,* provides a structural unity among the

2. Stoppard, " 'M' is for Moon Among Other Things," *TS*, p. 4.

otherwise disparate elements of the work. Alfred, for instance, dismisses his wife's encyclopedia because it lists only Monroe, James; not Monroe, Marilyn. There are also two surprising coincidences that substantiate the link between Constance and Monroe. Like Monroe, Constance was known by another name, Millie, until she decided it wasn't mature enough; and like Monroe, she takes pills to relieve her chronic insomnia. Through close association with a character as unglamorous and common as Constance, Monroe becomes a touchstone for the victim of contemporary society.

The second technique that appears in "'M' is for Moon," as well as several of the later works, is the revelation of a character's inner thoughts directly to the audience. Since this particular play was written expressly for radio, this form of direct address can readily be accomplished through a variety of technical devices. Although the thoughts of Alfred and Constance have little of the imaginative flow of the stream-of-consciousness monologue and even less of the rhetorical formality of the Elizabethan soliloquy, the premise of the play demands that their thoughts, however trivial or prosaic, be communicated to the audience.

Stoppard's experience in writing for radio undoubtedly sensitized him to the unique properties and possibilities inherent in that medium. But the peculiar ease with which radio (and television) can present a character's inner thoughts is a capability lost in naturalistic and realistic drama. Stoppard has repeatedly adapted that capability for the stage to establish counterpoint between dialogue and inner feelings. In *Night and Day*, for instance, a play written fourteen years later, Stoppard offers a distinction between Ruth Carson, as the character is identified when in contact with other characters, and "Ruth," the self-conscious internal voice that the audience—though not the other characters—can hear.

The woman character type foreshadowed by Constance does not reappear until *If You're Glad I'll Be Frank*; thereafter, beginning with Dorothy Moore in *Jumpers*, the type shows greater strength and culminates in the person of Ruth Carson. Stoppard's female protagonists typically verge on mental instability partially because they live in worlds dominated by men but also because they are over-whelmed by technology. For Constance, technology is rep-resented by the television whose steady drone allows Alfred to ignore her while imagining his liaison with Mari-lyn Monroe.

Stylistically "'M' is for Moon" is in many ways more like Stoppard's work in the 1970s, especially *Jumpers* and *Night and Day*, than the works with which it is linked by chronology. It confronts its audience with characters in a domestic situation but relies upon little of the naturalistic superstructure that characterizes his first full-length play, *Enter a Free Man*.

Enter a Free Man is a revised version of *A Walk on the Water*, which was broadcasted by Rediffusion in 1963. That it was televised only a day or two after the assassination of John F. Kennedy assured that its viewing audience would be small indeed ("Definite Maybe," p. 19). Stoppard began the play in 1960, but it was not published until 1968, the same year it was performed in London's West End.

Like several other contemporary British playwrights, Stoppard grounded his first full-length work in strong-ly conventional, representational characterization and dramaturgy. Like John Osborne's *Look Back in Anger* (1956), Robert Bolt's *Flowering Cherry* (1957), and Peter Shaffer's *Five Finger Exercise* (1958), *Enter a Free Man* is a domestic drama employing a contemporary setting and scarcely ven-turing outside the secure footing of representational drama. Each of these four playwrights, however, soon transgressed the boundaries of realism and naturalism: Osborne in *The Entertainer* (1957), Bolt in *A Man For All Seasons* (1960), Shaffer in *The Royal Hunt of the Sun* (1964), and Stoppard in virtually all of his subsequent work. Their departure from strictly representational drama indicates not simply a desire or willingness to experiment with new dramatic forms, but a conscious effort to recover the tra-ditional conventions of drama—the music-hall Chairman, the Elizabethan soliloquy, the Brechtian narrator, or the choric song. Especially in their use of vehicles that directly address the audience, these four dramatists violate the in-tegrity of the fourth wall and thereby undercut the essen-tial premise of representational drama. Moreover, there is a self-consciousness and an acute awareness of the dramatic traditions implicit in their dissatisfaction with the limitations of realism and naturalism. Osborne, Bolt, Shaffer, and, especially, Stoppard are all well versed in the history and traditions of drama; all appreciate the arbitrary and artificial restraints imposed on drama by representationalism.

That Stoppard has called *Enter a Free Man* "The Flowering Death of a Salesman" ("Ambushes," p. 4) is indicative of his indebtedness to both Arthur Miller and Robert Bolt. Indeed, the contradictions uttered by George Riley about his daughter (at one moment she is squandering her brains by working at Woolworth's, the next she is a shiftless idler) are immediately reminiscent of Willy Loman's ambivalence toward his sons. Her name, Linda, also recalls the wife in Miller's play. Although Stoppard continued to borrow (or steal) characters from other playwrights, he acknowledged that *Enter a Free Man* was a mechanical exercise:

> I don't think it's a very true play, in the sense that I feel no intimacy with the people I was writing about. It works pretty well as a play, but it's actually phoney because it's a play written about other people's characters.
>
> ("Ambushes," p. 5)

He has also said that *Enter a Free Man* "cleared the decks" ("Ambushes," p. 4)—suggesting that he purged himself of the influence of what he elsewhere called the "Meet the Family"[3] strain of contemporary drama. Indeed, with hindsight *Enter a Free Man* can be seen as his exorcism of the naturalistic impulse from his playwrighting. Balanced between the two stock settings of domestic drama, the living room and the bar, *Enter a Free Man* is bound to the character types, dialogue, and formulaic action that have dominated commercial theatre in this century.

Although the representational dramaturgy of *Enter a Free Man* contains very little of what will emerge as Stoppard's distinctive style, it does anticipate some of his recurrent substance. George, who fancies himself the free man of the play's ironic title, describes himself as "a creative

3. Stoppard, "New Wave Olivier," *Scene* 14 (12 December 1962): 44.

spirit,"[4] "a man standing on the brink of great things" (p. 32). Entirely dependent on others for food, spending money, cigarettes, and the fulfillment of his dreams, he is quick to identify himself as another Edison. But George's inventions are eminently impracticable if not downright ludicrous. He, however, is hopelessly oblivious of the drawbacks of a grandfather clock that (much to the consternation of his wife and daughter) plays "Rule Britannia" at noon and midnight, a water-cooled machine gun that also boils water for the soldier's tea, or a network of indoor plumbing that cannot be turned off. While not tinkering with some useless gismo, George plots his flight from his wife Persephone and daughter. His fantasies of escaping a family that has saddled him with "twenty-five years of dead domesticity" (p. 12), of fleeing to South America with a woman whom he knows only casually, and of starting a business with an unctuous acquaintance intend to elicit the respect of his drinking cronies and perhaps even the love of his family. Sadly everyone, on both sides of the stage, is wise to him.

But George is not the only character of *Enter a Free Man* who attempts to escape, however futilely, the tedium and vacuity of home life; his daughter runs off with her boyfriend only to face an analogous disillusionment. Linda's ill-fated elopement is foiled by a car accident and the revelation that her betrothed is already married. For both George and Linda, their dreams simply fail to materialize; glamour, fame, and success are neither imminent nor inevitable. Although Linda is her father's most candid and severe detractor ("He's living in dreamland" [p. 58] she tells her mother, anticipating Dorothy Moore's description of her husband in *Jumpers*), she is also very much his child and given to similar delusions. Her elaborately embellished descriptions of romantic encounters are perhaps more hyperbolic but equally illusory as her father's fantasies.

The parallels between Linda and George anticipate Stoppard's use of doubling in *Rosencrantz and Guildenstern*. Just as George and Linda are linked by their flight from the commonplace, Rosencrantz and Guildenstern are linked to

4. Stoppard, *Enter a Free Man* (London: Faber, 1968), p. 35.

the Tragedians on the basis of their game playing and their submission to a predetermined role. George (and to a lesser extent Linda) is the precursor of many of Stoppard's protagonists. Like Rosencrantz and Guildenstern, George Moore, Birdboot, and Carr, George sees himself on the brink of greatness. Although he senses this proximity, the audience knows he will fail to achieve it.

Theatrically, *Enter a Free Man* is perhaps the most unimaginative of Stoppard's works. Act 1 illustrates the formulation of George's and Linda's plans for escape to the better life they think is imminent; Act 2 presents their disillusionment and reluctant return to their routines. But *Enter a Free Man* lacks both the breathtaking theatrics that will appear in the later works and the insight that comes with true resolution. The play resembles Ibsen's *The Wild Duck* in its consideration of man's need for a life-lie, an illusion to sustain his dignity and self-respect (Hayman, p. 14). Whereas Ibsen clearly speaks for this human need, Stoppard poses the question of man's dependency on illusion but suggests no answer. Stoppard's refusal to accept or reject the value of a life-lie is wholly consistent with his ironic tone and his unwillingness, at least in the sixties, to moralize. From the sympathy with which George is depicted, the audience can infer that his fight is at least worth fighting, but that conclusion is tentative at best.

Enter a Free Man does contain, albeit in embryonic form, some of the techniques of characterization that will be used in Stoppard's later works. Early in Act 1 and again at the end of that act (the dialogue recurs verbatim), Linda speculates about what her father is like at his pub:

> He's got to be different—I mean you wouldn't even *know* me if you could see me—... And that goes for everyone. There's two of everyone. You see you need that and if the two of him's the same in the pub as he is with us, then he's had it.
>
> (pp. 10, 54)

Here Linda introduces the notion of two distinct sides of her father's personality. In at least three of the plays that follow *Enter a Free Man*, Stoppard juxtaposes the dual personalities of his protagonists, a contrast most evident in the character's use of language. In *Rosencrantz and Guildenstern*, the difference between the largely idiomatic speech of Ros and Guil when left to themselves and the Elizabethan dialogue of Shakespeare's play indicates the contrast between their unaffected personalities and the roles they assume at Elsinore. In *The Real Inspector Hound*, Birdboot, who rambles on in the journalistic cant that fills his reviews, is drawn into the play's main action by a phone call from his wife, Myrtle, an unexpected intrusion from his private life into his public persona. Once he lifts the receiver, Birdboot abandons the jargon as well as his role as a spectator and is immersed in the world of Muldoon Manor. Moreover, *Night and Day* offers the contrast between Ruth, the gracious hostess, and "Ruth," the self-critical cynic.

Finally, the setting of *Enter a Free Man* is noteworthy because of its use of multiple playing areas. Here the play's action is divided between Riley's living room and his neighborhood pub, a division indicative of George's private and public selves. The use of multiple playing areas appears in *Jumpers* (in which three areas—study, bedroom, and hall—are employed); *Travesties* (which is divided between Carr's apartment and the Zurich public library); *Every Good Boy Deserves Favor* (which uses a cell, offices, and a schoolroom); and *Night and Day*. In each instance, Stoppard achieves a counterpoint by playing off dialogue from one playing area against that from another. In *Enter a Free Man*, for example, this technique is used effectively at the opening of the play as Riley's entrance at the pub, when he says "Enter a free man!" is undercut by Linda's comment "Poor old Dad" (pp. 10, 54). The simultaneous action in multiple playing areas also helps to break down the fourth wall and to burst the confines of representational drama.

Whereas the television adaptation of *Enter a Free Man*, *A Walk on the Water*, was the first of Stoppard's work broadcasted, *A Separate Peace* was his first play written specifically for television. Televised in August 1966, the same month that *Rosencrantz and Guildenstern* was performed by students on the fringe of the Edinburgh Festival, it was also the first play in which John Wood, the actor for whom the part of Carr in *Travesties* was written, performed a Stoppard role.

John Brown, the protagonist of *A Separate Peace* and a man ostensibly as average as his name, has saved his money in order to retreat from the world at the Beechwood Nursing Home. Although untroubled by any physical malady, Brown seeks the refuge and regimentation of the nursing home as a rejection of the outside world; he asks only that nothing be expected of him. Baffled by the peculiar desire of this odd man, the resident doctor eventually discovers that Brown was once a patient in this same nursing home. Brown's quest for an environment where nothing is expected of him apparently dates from the time he was brought to Beechwood as a boy to recuperate from a car accident. Enchanted by the order, neatness, and totally relaxing atmosphere of the home, he has longed for its tranquility ever since he left.

While staying at the hospital, Brown befriends a young nurse, Maggie, to whom he explains his situation: "I came for the quiet and the routine. I came for the white calm, meals on trays and quiet efficiency, time passing and bringing nothing."[5] Brown also tells her that he did have "a good four years of it once" (p. 166); once, as it turns out, was the four years he spent as a prisoner of war. He tells her:

> The camp was like breathing out for the first time in months. I couldn't believe it. It was like winning, being captured. . . . The war was still going on but I wasn't going to it any more. They gave us food, life was regulated, in a box of earth and wire and sky, and sometimes you'd hear an aeroplane miles up, but it couldn't touch you. On my second day, I knew what it reminded me of. . . . It reminded me of here.
>
> (p. 168)

Like Rosencrantz and Guildenstern, Brown demonstrates a distinct preference to surrender his decisionmaking powers to someone or something else, even if it means living as a prisoner of war. As Brown tells us, what he is actually looking for is a "monastery for agnostics" (p. 170). Brown is fully aware of his dilemma. In the opening moments of

---

5. Stoppard, "A Separate Peace," in *Albert's Bridge and Other Plays* (New York: Grove, 1977), p. 156.

the work, he tells the hospital's doctor that he missed his connection (p. 110); in the final exchange between the doctor and Brown, the impossibility of his scheme is affirmed:

> BROWN (*angrily*): You couldn't leave well enough alone, could you?
> DOCTOR (*pause; not phoney any more*): It's not enough, Mr. Brown. You've got to... *connect*....
> (pp. 172–73)

Like Septimus Smith in Virginia Woolf's *Mrs. Dalloway*, John Brown misses his connection with life. Finally he is expelled from his Edenic refuge and returns to the confusion and turmoil of the outside world. Like Albert on his bridge, Brown's happiness is contingent upon his anonymous withdrawal from the havoc of modern life.

Escape is the ultimate aim of the protagonists of these three plays: Alfred of "'M' is for Moon" has his casual fantasies of intimate conversations with Marilyn Monroe; George has his carefully plotted pipedreams and inventions; John Brown his temporary respite from societal chaos. In his next works, Gladys Jenkins and Albert also seek refuge from a world that is too much for them. Rosencrantz and Guildenstern, however, refuse engagement with the world not by withdrawing from its trials but by abdicating control of their destiny to some other power—a king's will, fate, or perhaps simply chance. In even later works, Stoppard's protagonists still are curiously at odds with the worlds they inhabit. Irrespective of whether that world is a hyperbolic dystopia of the none-too-distant future or a comically exaggerated picture of Zurich during World War I, his more recent protagonists attempt to justify themselves rather than to withdraw.

The two radio plays, *If You're Glad I'll Be Frank* and *Albert's Bridge*, not only demonstrate Stoppard's ability to work specifically for the medium of radio but also advance the character type found in the earlier works. From his work in radio, the dramatic monologue will evolve as one of his staples and fortes.

Glad/Frank contains some of the most lyrical writing that Stoppard has ever produced. As Ronald Hayman notes, "Even if Stoppard was not directly influenced by

Four Quartets, his verse bears a certain resemblance to Eliot's both in its rhythms and the attitudes it expresses" (pp. 55–56). The poetic passages of *Glad/Frank* are restricted to the interior monologues of Gladys Jenkins, the woman whose voice announces the time over the telephone, not through technologically assisted means, but live—each and every time the time is given. As the speaking clock girl, Gladys finds security by withdrawing from a society whose pace she cannot tolerate but she also loses the warmth of human contact. The point is not simply that technology has further imprisoned rather than liberated Gladys, but that she has consciously chosen the anonymity and estrangement of the mechanically disembodied voice. Several times during the play, Gladys refers to her previous efforts to escape life's trivialities by joining a convent. When Gladys's superiors became aware of her lack of faith, she was turned back out into the world:

> I asked her to let me stay inside without being a proper nun, it made no difference to me, it was the serenity I was after, that and the clean linen, but she wasn't having any of that.[6]

Some time in Gladys's past she appears to have found comfort in her marriage to Frank, a remarkably amiable, ordinary bus driver whose dependability and punctuality suited both Gladys's temperament and the bus company's schedule.

Frank and Gladys share a passionate nature that belies their respective occupations' obsession with time and clockwork. In attempting to rescue Gladys from her apparent incarceration as the speaking clock, Frank tries to defy the system by stealing a few minutes from his timetable. Confronting both Gladys and Frank are a host of doormen and bureaucrats, cogs in the modern machine, who know all the rules—("You can't park there after seven if the month's got an R in it or before nine if it hasn't except on Christmas and the Chairman's birthday should it fall in Lent" [p. 58])—but who know nothing of passion.

The main contrast in the play, then, is between the

6. Stoppard, "If You're Glad I'll Be Frank," in *Albert's Bridge and Other Plays*, p. 62.

rhapsodic, allusive monologues of Gladys and the hollow prate of those from the allegedly real world. The latter is epitomized by the inane cant of the other telephone services (such as E-A-T, or dial-a-recipe: "Cheesey Croquets ... You will need a half pound of sharp Cheddar Cheese").[7] In contrast, Gladys sorts through her own mind in what we perceive as an ironic consideration of the nature of time:

> Because I wouldn't shake it off
> by going back, I'd only be in
> the middle of it,
> with an inkling of infinity,
> the only one who has seen both
>   ends
> rushing away from the middle.
> You can't keep your balance
>   after that.
> Because they don't know what
>   time is.
> They haven't experienced the
>   silence
> in which it passes
> impartial disinterested
> godlike.

(p. 53)

Gladys's perception of infinity is finally what shatters her sanity altogether. When her breakdown is discovered in the play's final scene, she explains this to Lord Coot, the First Lord of the Post Office: "At the third stroke I don't know what time it is and I don't care, because it doesn't go tick tock at all, it just goes and I have seen—I have seen infinity!" (p. 69). As for George Riley, Rosencrantz, and Guildenstern, there is no miraculous release for Gladys. But just as George fantasizes about escaping his domestic and financial failures by running off to South America and just as Rosencrantz and Guildenstern hope to avoid the fate revealed by the play's title, Gladys harbors the hope that Frank can rescue her from the system. In each in-

7. Stoppard, *If You're Glad I'll Be Frank*, rev. ed. for the stage (New York: Samuel French, 1978), p. 13.

stance, the situation proves inescapable: George ends up by sponging a few bob from his daughter; the English ambassador perfunctorily announces the deaths of Rosencrantz and Guildenstern; the First Lord of the Post Office coaxes Gladys back to her calm, methodical persona. But despite the lack of the conventional happy ending, *Glad/Frank* and *Albert's Bridge,* like Stoppard's other plays, are still primarily comic rather than tragic, partially because the audience, if not the characters, recognize the impossibility of successful flight. What these characters seek to escape is ubiquitous, a condition of life itself.

Although most of Stoppard's previous works illustrate the inability of his protagonists to escape death, failure, or the system, *Albert's Bridge* recalls *A Separate Peace* in depicting at least a momentarily successful flight. Like John Brown's retreat to a nursing home, Albert's withdrawal to the bridge is ultimately quashed, but not before he relishes the bliss of escaping society. Like Gladys and Brown, Albert finds he cannot abide the world and its inhabitants. Unlike the others, however, Albert had a materially comfortable life awaiting him as heir to his father's fortune, as president of Metal Alloys and Allied Metals. Had he only been willing to accept the social amenities his mother mandates and the regimen his father envisions, Albert would have settled into an easy albeit dull life. But some seed of discontent, perhaps sown in his philosophy classes at the university, has taken root in Albert, and by taking a summer job painting Clufton Bay Bridge, he renounces his parents' plans for him.

The lofty perspective from the bridge affords Albert a vision of an ordered and coherent world as well as an agreeable distance from the terrestrial matters of daily life. As Albert withdraws first from his parents and then from his wife and child, he grows to love his work in a way that few people can. Clufton Bay Bridge becomes not only the symbol of the town's prosperity but also the sole source of Albert's happiness. In the bridge's strength and geometrical symmetry, Albert discovers what philosophy had failed to offer him. As he says: "It's absurd, really, being up there, looking down on the university lying under you like a couple of bricks, full of dots studying philosophy—what could they possibly know? I saw more up there in three weeks than those dots did in three years. I saw the context."[8] By placing his faith in and directing his energies toward his work, Albert comes to admire the solidity and fixity of the bridge that stand in contrast to the flux and flow of human relationships.

His internal monologues, soliloquies while at work on the bridge, reveal a contemplative soul that he is either unable or unwilling to express in dealing with others. Like Gladys, he contemplates the nature of time and the question of perspective. His work gives him a sense of permanence (which is in itself ironic because the paint continually deteriorates) as well as purpose. He has, in fact, found his place and imagines himself spending the rest of his life painting the bridge:

> Dip brush, dip brush
> without end, come rain or shine;
> A fine way to spend my time.
> My life is set out for me,
> the future traced in brown,
> my past measured in silver;
> how absurd, how sublime.

(p. 23)

> ... in eight years I'll be pushing thirty-two
> a manic painter coming through for the second time.

(p. 38)

As his devotion to the bridge grows, his antipathy to all else also increases: he becomes disenchanted with his wife and their child. Moreover, when human contact, in the person of Fraser, threatens his solitude he responds first by urging the intruder to carry out his planned suicide and then by protesting to his superiors.

Fraser and Albert both enjoy the detachment afforded them by the height of the bridge because each is, as Fraser describes himself, "a victim of perspective" (p. 37):

> Down there I am assailed by the flying splinters of a world breaking up at the speed of procreation without end. The

8. Stoppard, "Albert's Bridge," in *Albert's Bridge and Other Plays*, p. 17.

centre cannot hold and the outside edge is filling out like a balloon, without the assurance of infinity. More men are hungry than honest, and more eat than produce. The apocalypse cannot be long delayed.

(pp. 38–39)

Fraser's propensity for poetry, and even philosophy, is shared with Albert, but their primary similarity is the serenity both feel when viewing the world from the bridge. They are, like all of Stoppard's characters, ultimately unsuccessful in their flight from the world. The play ends as an army of painters, intent on completing Albert's work, marches on to the bridge in step and thereby collapses it. Albert's final observation, made as his death appears imminent, is: "To go to such lengths! I didn't do them any harm! What did I have that they wanted?" (p. 41). What he had, of course, was what John Brown, Gladys Jenkins, and many other Stoppard characters all seek—certainty and seclusion.

These early plays establish the betrayal of expectations as one of Stoppard's favorite devices. The regimentation of John Brown's P.O.W. camp, the geometrical symmetry and solidity of Albert's bridge, and the monotony of Gladys's job are not drawbacks but attractions. Repetition, tedium, and unremitting sameness are exactly what these characters seek. Certainty—even if it means imprisonment—is preferable to chaos. Similarly, Rosencrantz and Guildenstern, as well as the Tragedians, demonstrate a clear preference for conforming to a predetermined role over making their own way in a world that offers few certitudes.

Stoppard's recurrent character type clearly evolves from the protagonists of these early works. Their persistence in spite of failure and against overwhelming odds, their tangential connection with fame and greatness, their ironic self-detachment foreshadow their more mature and fully developed counterparts in the later plays. Their concern with the relativity of perspective is a theme that will resonate throughout Stoppard's mature work.

Stylistically, Stoppard narrows his range during his period of apprenticeship by recognizing drama (whether for radio, television, or the stage) rather than fiction as his métier. Throughout his career, he will continue to experiment in various media, demonstrating his versatility but also anticipating his adaptation of certain devices, such as the voice-over, from radio and television to stage performance. His use of the dramatic monologue in " 'M' is for Moon Among Other Things," *If You're Glad I'll Be Frank,* and *Albert's Bridge* are essential forerunners in the development of the interior voices of his later protagonists—notably George Moore, Henry Carr, and Ruth Carson. In his evolution as a playwright, Stoppard will continue to experiment with dramatic styles, ranging from naturalism to farce, but just as he deserted fiction for drama, he will abandon naturalism to pursue his distinctive dramatic style.

Most of these early works are hardly works of genius. Often they are shackled to a dramaturgy that cannot accommodate Stoppard's impulse toward theatricalism and verbal pyrotechnics. Sometimes their ideas are limited to the small minds of their protagonists. Nonetheless, they are important prefigurations of the thematic and stylistic concerns that will emerge with increasing clarity in Stoppard's plays of the late sixties and seventies.

III

T he success of *Rosencrantz and Guildenstern Are Dead* both in Edinburgh and London depended upon a single dazzling review among a host of unenthusiastic notices. Ronald Bryden in the *Observer* lavished praise upon the play as presented in Edinburgh, and Harold Hobson in the *Sunday Times* called the 1967 production in London "the most important event in the British professional theatre of the last nine years" (that is, as Tynan points out, since the opening of Pinter's *The Birthday Party*).[1] As with Osborne's *Look Back in Anger*, the superlatives with which one critic greeted the play triggered a ground swell of excitement. *Rosencrantz and Guildenstern* brought Stoppard the *Evening Standard* Award for Most Promising Playwright (shared with David Storey), the Best Play Award from *Plays and Players*, and the John Whiting Award.

The history of the composition of *Rosencrantz and Guildenstern* belies the notion that Stoppard systematically mined *Hamlet* to exploit the thematic coincidences between his play and Shakespeare's. Stoppard's work began as a one-act play that dealt only roughly with what is now its text. While in Germany in 1964, studying on a grant from the Ford Foundation, Stoppard wrote a one-act verse burlesque entitled *Rosencrantz and Guildenstern Meet King Lear*. The final version of *Rosencrantz and Guildenstern* "owes little to the one-acter except momentum."[2] Two years later, a second version, the first titled *Rosencrantz and Guildenstern Are Dead*, was offered as a fringe presentation at the Edinburgh Festival by the Oxford Theatre Group. In 1965, the Royal Shakespeare Company took a twelve-month option on the play. But this version, too, was substantially revised before the play was performed by the National Theatre. Stoppard himself recalls that "I wrote an entirely new scene for London," largely because in the read-through of

---

1. Tynan is particularly generous to Pinter because, more likely, Hobson refers to Tynan's own bellwether review of Osborne's *Look Back in Anger* in the *Observer* in 1956.
2. Taylor, *The Angry Theatre* (New York: Hill and Wang, 1969), p. 319.

the play with the literary managers of the National Theatre (Laurence Olivier and Kenneth Tynan), Olivier pointed out that Stoppard had omitted an entire scene from *Hamlet* in which Rosencrantz and Guildenstern appear (*Transatlantic Review*, p. 18).

Paradoxically, two of Stoppard's best and most original works, *Rosencrantz and Guildenstern* and *Travesties*, are also his most highly derivative works. In these plays, the overt borrowing of the characters, plots, and dialogue from Shakespeare's *Hamlet* and Wilde's *The Importance of Being Earnest* evinces not only Stoppard's conscious acknowledgment of his dramatic forebears but also his appeal to a self-conscious, elitist audience. Moreover, the highly derivative nature of these specific plays and Stoppard's canon in general is a quality he shares with Shakespeare and Wilde. Kyd's *Ur-Hamlet* predates Shakespeare's most famous play, and Wilde's masterpiece stands as the culmination of nineteenth-century farce rather than as the cornerstone for British comedy in this century. Finally, the highly derivative nature of these works allies Stoppard with numerous other contemporary playwrights, notably Edward Bond, Jean Anouilh, Bertolt Brecht, and Jean Giraudoux, who have also chosen to rely upon the traditions of drama for their plot, characters, and settings. The derivative quality and elitist appeal of *Rosencrantz and Guildenstern* have not damaged the popularity of Stoppard's most famous work, largely because it is, at least on one level, self-contained. It can be appreciated by viewers who know of *Hamlet* but who do not know *Hamlet*'s themes.

Critics, however, often slight Stoppard's debt to Shakespeare and instead emphasize his indebtedness to Samuel Beckett and absurdist theatre. Stoppard suggested that the connection between himself and Beckett

> is the easiest to make, yet the most deceptive. Most people who say Beckett mean *Waiting for Godot*. They haven't read his novels, for example. I can see a lot of Beckettian things in all my work, but they're not actually to do with the image of two lost souls waiting for something to happen, which is why most people connect *Rosencrantz* with *Waiting for Godot*, because they had this scene in common . . . I wasn't thinking so much of what they are about so much as the way in which

Beckett expresses himself, and the bent of his humour. I find Beckett deliciously funny in the way that he qualifies everything as he goes along, reduces, refines and dismantles.

(*Transatlantic Review*, p. 20)

But most critics who have linked Stoppard with the Theatre of the Absurd have stressed other connections. John Russell Taylor, for instance, asserts that from the very beginning of *Rosencrantz*, "we know immediately that we are in that pale region of Theatre of the Absurd where knockabout and arid philosophical speculation alternate while the awaited never comes."[3] Jill Levenson argues that Stoppard's plays are characterized by "features peculiar to the Theatre of the Absurd as Martin Esslin has described it" (p. 431).

Psychologically, Ros and Guil (Stoppard's abbreviated nicknames for the characters) are just as delicately balanced, as dominant and submissive, as are Beckett's Vladimir and Estragon. They are perhaps less quarrelsome than what many have identified as their French prototypes but equally interdependent. Moreover, they share with Vladimir and Estragon a love of game playing and a tenuous grip on the past.

The language of *Rosencrantz* illustrates Stoppard's eclectic borrowing from absurdist drama. Its discursive and even conversational language clearly distinguishes it from the Theatre of the Absurd. But many of the exchanges between Ros and Guil, rooted one moment in clichés to ward off silence, the next in word game, the next in the formality of lofty philosophical speculation, evoke what Eugene Ionesco calls the "tragedy of language." But when this same dialogue is compared with that of Stoppard's compatriot and contemporary, Harold Pinter, the conversations between Ros and Guil seem nearly naturalistic. Upon closer scrutiny, all the dialogue in the play can be seen as sequentially linked and logically grounded. What some have identified as absurdist dialogue can reasonably be viewed as idiosyncratic conversation between two intimate friends; it is filled with the shorthand of in-jokes and

3. Martin Esslin, *The Theatre of the Absurd*, rev. ed. (Garden City, N.Y.: Anchor, 1969), p. 6.

shared experiences. In its essence the dialogue of *Rosencrantz and Guildenstern* is not absurdist.

In addition to the discursiveness of its language the central points that distinguish Stoppard's play from the Theatre of the Absurd are, stylistically, its dogged albeit qualified reliance upon logic and causality; and, thematically, its refusal to submit to despair. Martin Esslin, who coined the term *Theatre of the Absurd,* and who makes no mention of Stoppard in his 1969 revision of his study, specifies that "the Theatre of the Absurd strives to express its sense of the senselessness of the human condition and the inadequacy of the rational approach by the open abandonment of rational devices and discursive thought."[4] Even though Ros and Guil obviously abuse and manipulate logic, it provides the basis of their games and of the play's action. At the outset of the play, Guil, having lost ninety coins to Ros, logically and methodically seeks to rationalize his incredibly bad luck:

> One: I'm willing it. Inside where nothing shows, I am the essence of a man spinning double-headed coins, and betting against himself in private atonement for an unremembered past. . . . Two: time has stopped dead and the single experience of one coin being spun once has been repeated ninety times . . . On the whole, doubtful. Three: divine intervention, that is to say, a good turn from above concerning him, cf. children of Israel, or retribution from above concerning me, cf. Lot's wife. Four: a spectacular vindication of the principle that each individual coin spun individually is as likely to come down heads as tails and therefore should cause no surprise each individual time it does.[5]

Among these possibilities, the second, that time has stopped dead, is the only one endemic to the Theatre of the Absurd and the only one discounted by Guil. The audience's awareness of the passage of time, moreover, is corroborated by the forward-moving action of the play.

4. Stoppard, *Rosencrantz and Guildenstern Are Dead* (New York: Grove, 1967), p. 16.

5. See p. 114. That Stoppard identifies the emergence of the Tragedians from the barrels as "impossible" suggests a conscious manipulation of the conventions of realistic drama.

Rosencrantz is an entirely sequential play. Despite the anachronistic umbrella and language, as well as the admittedly impossible stage direction of Act 3, its action is not only sequential but also governed by causality. As in the ostensibly absurd tableau that opens *After Magritte,* Stoppard takes great pains to offer logically plausible although improbable explanations of what transpires in *Rosencrantz.*

But even beyond the comparatively causal and sequential dramaturgy of *Rosencrantz,* the philosophical implications of the play are far removed from those of absurdist drama. The vision of the Theatre of the Absurd is predicated upon the hopelessness, meaninglessness, and futility of the human condition. However laugh-provoking the plays of Beckett and Ionesco may be, their comedy is undercut by the despair that is implicit in the portrayal of man; that laughter is, in fact, recognition of the emptiness and senselessness of life. There is no such bleak perception of mankind's condition, no angst, no despair lurking beneath the surface of *Rosencrantz,* or even of Stoppard's other works.

The dominant structural pattern that Stoppard employs in *Rosencrantz* is doubling. Throughout the play, the audience, other characters, and even Ros and Guil themselves have difficulty in distinguishing the two attendant lords. The text of the play seems to offer clearer distinctions between Ros and Guil than many stage productions. From the outset, we observe that one (Ros) is an apparently habitual winner while the other (Guil) is plagued by a run of very bad luck. Stoppard's stage direction specifies that:

> The run of "heads" is impossible, yet ROS betrays no surprise at all—he feels none. However, he is nice enough to feel a little embarrassed at taking so much money off his friend. Let that be his character note. GUIL is well alive to the oddity of it. He is not worried about the money, but he is worried by the implications; aware but not going to panic about it—his character note.
>
> (p. 11)

But neither character is mentioned by name until the arrival of the Tragedians, and then Ros mistakenly introduces himself as Guil. Ros is consistently less introspective and more intuitive than Guil. On the other hand, Guil is more expansive, contemplative, and speculative; at times he even seems to foreshadow the George Moore of *Jumpers*. Guil's consideration of his own mortality in Act 3 anticipates both the style of Moore's composition of a philosophical defense (in that Guil might well be speaking to an imaginary mirror fixed in an imaginary fourth wall) and Moore's substance (or lack thereof):

> Well, yes, and then again no. (*Airily*.) Let us keep things in proportion. Assume, if you like, that they're going to kill him [Hamlet]. Well, he is a man, he is mortal, death comes to us all, etcetera, and consequently he would have died anyway, sooner or later. Or to look at it from the social point of view—he's just one man among many, the loss would be well within reason and convenience. And then, again, what is so terrible about death? As Socrates so philosophically put it, since we don't know what death is, it is illogical to fear it.
> (p. 110)

Like Moore, Guil never lets his subject rest in a fixed position; instead, he circles it and appraises it from various vantage points. In these techniques, Guil incorporates two of Stoppard's favorite themes: the limitations inherent in approaching a subject from a fixed perspective and the notion that his characters "play a sort of infinite leapfrog" ("Ambushes," p. 5). Here Guil offers not only arguments but also his own refutation, a rebuttal of the refutation, and then a counter-rebuttal.

Ros's and Guil's love of game playing, shared by George and Dorothy Moore in *Jumpers*, begins in Act 1 with their coin-flipping and their game of questions in which syllogisms, repetitions, and rhetoric are fouls. In Act 2, Ros reports their disastrous attempt to "glean what afflicts" Hamlet through this same game of questions. (Although we have no reason to suspect that Hamlet was aware of the rules of that game, he outscored them twenty-seven to three [p. 57].) By the play's final act, Ros's and Guil's game playing ostensibly gives way to action as they are confronted with the fact of their shameless manipulation by Claudius, impending doom, and pirates. Near

39

the very end of the play, Guil is at last galvanized into taking action in his attempt to kill the Player. Driven by a need to assert that he is alive and capable of action, quite capable in fact of transcending the artificiality of game playing, Guil stabs the Player in a serious attempt to murder him. The final twist, the last laugh that existence has upon Guil, however, is that even in this—what is for him an extreme act of rebellion through violence—he finds himself trapped in a world of games; the Player's knife turns out to be only a collapsing prop for playing death on the stage. Philosophically, this moment is as close as *Rosencrantz* ever comes to the despair of the Theatre of the Absurd.

By this point in the play, the structural pattern of doubling includes extensive parallels between Ros and Guil on the one hand and the Tragedians on the other, between the game playing of the former and the playacting of the latter. The initial encounter between Ros and Guil and the actors establishes this analogy between Shakespeare's play and Stoppard's:

> It is this metaphor that Stoppard has borrowed in his transposition of Hamlet—the Elizabethan noble hero—into Ros and Guil—the modern nonentities... But unlike Hamlet, who manages to achieve some dignity within the limits of his role, Ros and Guil succumb to the play-life metaphor, still limited in their minor roles.[6]

Indeed, Anne Righter's comments on playacting in *Hamlet* in *Shakespeare and the Idea of the Play* seem equally applicable to *Rosencrantz*:

> It is dominated by the idea of the play. In the course of its development the play metaphor appears in a number of forms. It describes the dissembler, the Player King, the difference between appearance and reality, falsehood and truth, and the theatrical nature of certain moments of time. The relationship of world and stage is reciprocal: the actor holds a mirror up to nature, but the latter in its turn reflects the features of the play.[7]

6. William Babula, "The Play-Life Metaphor in Shakespeare and Stoppard," *Modern Drama* 13 (1970): 280.

7. Anne Righter, *Shakespeare and the Idea of the Play* (Baltimore: Penguin, 1967), p. 142.

Through the use of the play metaphor in regard to the troupe of Tragedians who follow Rosencrantz and Guildenstern, Stoppard establishes the relationship between spectator and player. Like the pair of courtiers, the actors have welded their fortunes together, as revealed when the Player loses his coins to Guildenstern. The Player, like Guildenstern, is the most vocal of his group and, hence, its collective spokesman. Just as Ros and Guil are unable to remember even the previous day, the Player speaks of the Tragedians' tenuous grip on memory and the past when he, echoing Beckett's Pozzo, says, "by this time tomorrow we might have forgotten everything we ever knew" (p. 22).

Early in the play, the Player, in speaking to Ros, indicates the relationship between action on the stage and in real life: "We do on stage things that are supposed to happen off. Which is a kind of integrity, if you look on every exit being an entrance somewhere else" (p. 28). Indeed, even the dumb show the Tragedians perform before the court at Elsinore parallels the action of Stoppard's play, albeit with a curious twist: whereas their performance is action without speech, that of Ros and Guil is speech without action. After the dumb show and the Tragedians' play, Guil heartily objects to their presentation, arguing that the melodramatic depiction of death is not faithful to reality. He tells the Player:

> No, no, no . . . you've got it all wrong . . . you can't act death. The *fact* of it is nothing to do with seeing it happen—it's not gasps and blood and falling about—that isn't what makes it death. It's just a man failing to reappear, that's all—now you see him, now you don't, that's the only thing that's real: here one minute and never coming back—an exit, unobtrusive and unannounced, gathering weight as it goes on, until, finally, it is heavy with death.
>
> (p. 84)

What Guil perceives as the unreality of the performance not only leaves him incapable of recognizing the applicability of the dumb show to his own life but also foreshadows his death at the end of Stoppard's play. Even at the end of *Hamlet*, the Ambassador only announces the deaths of

Rosencrantz and Guildenstern; the audience simply sees them disappear, not die.

On several occasions, Ros and Guil step to the apron of the stage and obliquely acknowledge the presence of the audience. In Act 2, for instance, Ros breaks the fourth wall as he plays upon the audience's assumption of the unreality of stage action:

> ROS *leaps up and bellows at the audience.*
> ROS: Fire!
> GUIL *jumps up.*
> GUIL: Where?
> ROS: It's all right—I'm demonstrating the misuse of free speech. To prove that it exists. (*He regards the audience, that is the direction, with contempt—and other directions, then front again.*) Not a move. They should burn to death in their shoes.
> (p. 60)

Both Guil's objection to the Player's portrayal of death and Ros's demonstration of the misuse of free speech demonstrate their consciousness of the conventions of playacting and of offering a performance; both of these are points that reinforce the connection between Ros and Guil and the actors.

At the rehearsal of the Tragedians' play and again on board the ship to England, Ros and Guil are confronted not only with the actors, but with their precise doubles. In the former instance, the stage directions are unequivocal:

> The whole mime has been fluid and continuous, but now ROS moves forward and brings it to a pause. What brings ROS forward is the fact that under their cloaks the two SPIES are wearing coats identical to those worn by ROS and GUIL, whose coats are now covered by their cloaks. ROS approaches "his" SPY doubtfully. He does not quite understand why the coats are familiar.
> (p. 82)

These Spies are, of course, Stoppard's own invention; they do not appear in *Hamlet*. They confirm the strongest and most telling coincidence between the Tragedians and Ros and Guil, a coincidence that in turn establishes the link between Stoppard and Pirandello. Like the six characters searching for their author and like the Tragedians, Ros and Guil are bound to a script. While that script is familiar to the audience and even to the Tragedians, (at least as the plot of *The Murder of Gonzago*, the play within the play), it is unknown to Ros and Guil. As for Pirandello's six characters, the existence of Ros and Guil depends upon their being cast in a part by someone else. They freely surrender their ability to make decisions to some other agency—to the throne of Denmark that summons and commissions them; to the laws of chance that dictate a run of ninety-two consecutive heads; to anyone but themselves. They are, in fact, employed by Claudius and Gertrude for the identical reasons that the actors are employed by Hamlet; and the nature of that employment, playacting, is shared with the Tragedians.

Despite the presence of the two Spies, Ros and Guil fail to appreciate either the business of the actors or their own situation. At the rehearsal in Act 2, the Player explains this to Guil:

> PLAYER: Between "just desserts" and "tragic irony" we are given quite a lot of scope for our particular talent. Generally speaking, things have gone as far as they can possibly go when things have got about as bad as they reasonably get. (*He switches on a smile.*)
> GUIL: Who decides?
> PLAYER (*switching off his smile*): *Decides*? It is *written.*
> ... We're tragedians, you see. We follow directions—there is no *choice* involved. The bad end unhappily, the good unluckily. That is what tragedy means.
>
> (pp. 79–80)

The Player's definition of tragedy derives from Miss Prism's definition of fiction in Wilde's *The Importance of Being Earnest*: "The good end happily, and the bad unhappily. That is what Fiction means." Just as tragedy rather than fiction is the Player's subject, so the actors in Stoppard's play are called Tragedians rather than players. But the crucial distinction between Ros and Guil and the Tragedians lies in the fact that the latter group is fully conscious of surrendering their free will to a fixed text while Ros and Guil delude themselves with their games, logic, and hope that they can make sense of their situation.

Perhaps the closest Ros and Guil come to appreciating their own dilemma before being confronted with their impending deaths is in Act 1 when Guil argues:

> But we are comparatively fortunate; we might have been left to sift the whole field of human nomenclature, like two blind men looting a bazaar for their own portraits.

(p. 39)

The irony is, of course, that the image of blind men searching for their own images is immediately applicable to the situation of Ros and Guil. The image is, in fact, central to the play for it not only corroborates the extensive doubling pattern but also summons up the existential aphorism that existence precedes essence. The misplaced optimism of Ros and Guil rests in their hope that they may, like the blind men at the bazaar, find their identities in roles prescribed by someone other than themselves.

The play metaphor is the most important but clearly not the only connection between *Hamlet* and *Rosencrantz and Guildenstern*. Although the absurdist bent of Stoppard's work may seem to trivialize the plight of Ros and Guil by making it seem ludicrous or to deprecate the dramatic integrity of *Hamlet*'s characters, there are a number of substantial thematic links between Shakespeare's work and Stoppard's. Like Hamlet, Ros and Guil are distinctly uncomfortable in Denmark. Hamlet's uneasiness stems from the contrast between the reigns of Claudius and that of Hamlet's father as epitomized in his speech: "Though I am native here and to the manner born, it is a custom more honored in the breach than in the observance." (1.4.14–16). Hamlet repeatedly turns to Horatio as the one person in whom he can confide and place his trust. Similarly, Ros and Guil have only each other. This loneliness and estrangement triggers a series of further thematic coincidences between Shakespeare and Stoppard. Hamlet frequently considers the nature and even the desirability of death ("O that this too sullied flesh would melt..." [1.2.129]; "To be or not to be...." [3.1. 56]; To sleep, perchance to dream..." [3.1.60]). Ros and Guil also speculate about death's nature. Guil insists that death is not the histrionics of the Tragedians, but rather "just a man failing to reappear, that's all—now you see him now you don't, that's the only thing that's real" (p. 84). Unlike Hamlet, whose development as a character takes him from a melancholy obsession with death to an abandon predicated on his conviction that "readiness is all," Ros and particularly Guil move from freewheeling adventurousness to somber philosophizing. By the third act of *Rosencrantz and Guildenstern* both are preoccupied with the idea of death:

> ROS: We might as well be dead. Do you think death could possibly be a boat?
> GUIL: No, no, no . . . Death is . . . not. Death isn't. You take my meaning. Death is the ultimate negative. Not-being. You can't not-be on a boat.
> ROS: I've frequently not been on boats.
>
> (p. 108)

Ros's final comment, typical of his flippancy, undercuts the seriousness of Guil's speculations.

Like Hamlet, Ros and Guil are young men with an education but without a secure place at court or in the world. Many critics see Hamlet as besieged by vacillation, but Ros's and Guil's indecisiveness far exceeds the Prince of Denmark's. Although more trusting and hence more easily manipulated by Claudius, Ros and Guil share considerable common ground with Hamlet. They can even be seen as mid-twentieth-century analogues for the tragic character that Hamlet presented to the early seventeenth century.

The Real Inspector Hound was Stoppard's second play to reach West End audiences; it opened at the Criterion Theatre on 17 June 1968. The reviews were generally favorable but somewhat critical of the overtly farcical nature of the work. It was to be the only Stoppard work performed in the West End between 1967 and 1972.

Hound is indicative not only of Stoppard's experience as a drama critic but also of the venerable British tradition of theatrical whodunnits. If *Rosencrantz and Guildenstern* was Stoppard's homage to and attempt to handle what he has called "the most famous play in any language . . . part of a sort of common mythology" (*Transatlantic Review*, p. 19), *Hound* is his parodic salute to the continuing vigor and durability of a considerably less sophisticated but no less popular genre. Both works are overtly derivative and particularly dependent upon audience familiarity with the play's forebears. The expectations that the audience brings to *Hound* are clearly more important than the events that transpire at Muldoon Manor. As in *Rosencrantz*, Stoppard here demonstrates a clear willingness to consciously manipulate audience reaction—principally by establishing the validity of the conventions of drama (specifically those concerning the whodunnit) and then flagrantly violating them. Although Stoppard largely succeeded in exorcising his impulse toward domestic naturalism in *Enter a Free Man*, his attraction toward Shakespeare and the whodunnit persists long after *The Real Inspector Hound* and *Rosencrantz*.

The second point of coincidence between *Hound* and *Rosencrantz* is that both plays rely upon a dual structure analogous to that of the play within the play. As *Rosencrantz* recapitulates the most important themes of *Hamlet* (playacting, the conflicting claims of fate as opposed to free will, the meaning of death), so the various planes of action in *Hound* are first superimposed and eventually inextricably enmeshed. On the first plane, which is at first presented in realistic fashion, are the four drama critics: Birdboot, Moon, Higgs, and Puckeridge; the second plane gives us the characters and activities of the play set, as Mrs. Drudge obligingly informs us, in "the country residence of Lady Muldoon one morning in early spring."[8] But, more importantly, there is another level of action, closer still to the truth, which reveals the private lives of both the drama critics and the actors. While the stereotypical inhabitants of Muldoon Manor are obviously stilted, trite caricatures creaking under the weight of the whodunnit's formulas, the drama critics by striking their poses carry similar burdens. The postures of Moon and Birdboot are as contrived

8. Stoppard, *The Real Inspector Hound* (New York: Grove, 1969), p. 15.

and well planned as those of the characters in the play within the play. Hence, when the time finally comes to resolve the mysteries that exist on all three levels, the affected poses governing the behavior of the characters must yield.

To further convolute matters or at least to underscore the fact that the play works on several different levels, Stoppard specifies that the audience be "confronted by their own reflection in a huge mirror" (p. 7), a feat of stage design he admits is impossible but, however realized, is intended to raise the question of the relationship between art and reality, between drama and life. But the question is only raised—no attempt is made to answer it definitively. The answers provided by the play are feats of sleight of hand and suggest, if anything, that life is filled with petty jealousies, domestic infidelities, and banal emotional excesses.

Hound begins with the formal exposition concerning the first two planes of action—that of the drama critics and that of the whodunnit. At least initially the fourth wall of representational drama neatly cordons off these two planes as mutually exclusive. The substance of the play within the play at Muldoon Manor is familiar schlock: A man has been murdered but neither his identity nor his corpse has been discovered. Likewise, the story of Moon and Birdboot is a hackneyed tale of thwarted ambition and missed opportunities. In spite of the fact that the audience can see the body lying at center stage and hears Moon and Birdboot begin the play by questioning the whereabouts of Higgs, the naturalistic superstructure predisposes the audience to maintain the distinction between the two playing areas.

Hound is, in fact, replete with foreshadowings, tidbits of dramatic irony, indicative of the play's resolution. In the opening exchange between Birdboot and Moon, Birdboot asks no fewer than four times "where's Higgs?" (pp. 8–10). Higgs is, of course, right before their very eyes—the lifeless corpse at center stage. In that same conversation, Moon dodges Birdboot's assertion that the play at Muldoon Manor is a thriller, a "Who-killed thing" (p. 9), by responding, "I suppose so. Underneath." Underneath, that is all *The Real Inspector Hound* will prove to be as well.

Moon's subsequent lines, revealing him to be "more of a Cassandra-like figure than he realizes,"[9] prophesy his own death: "here lies Moon the second string, where's Higgs?" (p. 10); "I think I must be waiting for Higgs to die. ... Half-afraid that I will vanish when he does" (p. 18); "I'd still have Puckeridge behind *me* ... And if I could, so could he ... Uneasy lies the head that wears the crown" (p. 41).

Birdboot's and Moon's conversations have almost nothing to do with the play they have been sent to review. Birdboot's romantic affections shift from the actress playing Felicity to the one playing Cynthia; Moon dwells on Puckeridge, speculating that Puckeridge must be as envious of him as he is of Higgs. Both are obsessed with what they do: Birdboot, once on stage to answer Myrtle's telephone call, assumes that the actress Cynthia might well be enraptured with him ("Yes, well, a man of my influence is not to be sneezed at—I think I have some small name for the making of reputations—[p. 45]). Moon, by trying desperately to write a glowing account of an inconsequential play, attempts to assert that Higgs is not the only critic from his paper sent to cover important openings. Hence, Moon can argue that:

> If we examine this more closely, and I think close examination is the least tribute that this play deserves, I think we will find that within the austere framework of what is seen to be on one level a country-house week-end, and what a useful symbol that is, the author has given us—yes, I will go so far—he has given us the human condition—
>
> (p. 42)

What Ionesco called "the tragedy of language" works on all levels of *Hound*. As Crossley notes: "the critical language they [Moon and Birdboot] use throughout merely echoes the hackneyed dialogue of the play they review. The fact of their actual involvement on stage thereafter is, in effect, an extension in deed of their semantic complicity" (p. 79). Most of the conversations between Moon and

9. Brian M. Crossley, "An Investigation of Stoppard's *Hound* and Foot," *Modern Drama* 20 (1977): 80.

Birdboot are, in fact, not conversations at all, but separate monologues that take no account of what the other party has said or will say. In one pair of monologues, for instance, Birdboot defends himself against charges of philandering (of which he is guilty but as yet unaccused) while Moon ponders Puckeridge's envy. Neither is interested in listening to the other regardless of whether they speak of private or professional affairs. (Ironically, by the end of the play their private and professional lives fuse.)

Stoppard notes that Moon and Birdboot both "have a 'public' voice, a critic voice which they turn on for sustained pronouncements of opinion" (p. 21). But once Birdboot is smitten by the actress playing Cynthia and especially after he and Moon take the stage, the critical voice overtakes Birdboot entirely. Each loves to hear himself talk; each marvels at the selection of what he thinks is *le bon mot*. Their reviews rely upon the worst kind of psychological interpretations ("The son she never had, now projected in this handsome stranger and transformed into lover" [p. 25]), banality ("Trim-buttocked, that's the word for her" [p. 31]), and tautology ("*Je suis*, it seems to be saying, *ergo sum*" [p. 32]). Blinded to the fatuity and vacuity of their language they anticipate Milne's comment on journalists in general in *Night and Day:*

> People think that rubbish-journalism is produced by men of discrimination who are vaguely ashamed of truckling to the lowest taste. But it's not. It's produced by people doing their best work. [10]

Birdboot's vanity extends to carrying around with him a pocket slide viewer in which he shows Moon his entire review reproduced in neon outside the Theatre Royal. Moon then, to show his appreciation, appraises Birdboot's reproduced review with the same style, language, and gusto that he uses in reviewing plays:

> Yes ... yes ... lovely ... awfully sound. It has scale, it has color, it is, in the best sense of the word, electric. Large as it is, it is a small masterpiece—I would go so far as to say—

10. Stoppard, *Night and Day* (London: Faber, 1978), p. 6.

kinetic without being pop and having said that, I think it must be said that here we have a review that adds a new dimension to the critical scene. I urge you to make haste to the Theatre Royal, for this is the stuff of life itself.

(p. 15)

But even at this early point in the play, when the neon reproduction of a review of another play that may or may not have had anything to do with life itself is called "the stuff of life itself," the irony of "real" in *Hound*'s title is heightened.

In style as well as parodic temperament, Stoppard's play within the play bears striking resemblance to Joe Orton's *Loot* (1966) and, to a lesser extent, *What the Butler Saw* (1967). In both *Loot* and *Hound,* for instance, the audience sees the victim's corpse while some of the characters on stage remain oblivious to it; both plays show an allegedly formidable detective stumbling through his investigations; both demonstrate that guilt and the attendant fear of exposure govern the behavior of the play's characters whether they are guilty of the specific offense investigated by the detective or of some other crime. But Orton shows that everyone is guilty or at least complicit whereas Stoppard never ventures a moral about the universality of criminal behavior.

The character of the threatening yet bumbling police detective not only links Stoppard and Orton but also connects *The Real Inspector Hound* with *After Magritte.* First performed at the Ambiance Lunch-Hour Theatre Club on 9 April 1970, *After Magritte* is the first of Stoppard's works specifically written for an experimental company clearly outside the mainstream of Shaftsbury Avenue. Subsequently, Stoppard wrote a number of plays for Inter-Action, a company founded in 1971 that survived the decade largely because several of Britain's best playwrights (Harold Pinter, Heathcote Williams, James Saunders, as well as Stoppard) have developed scripts specifically for it. Among Stoppard's other works for Inter-Action are *Dogg's Our Pet* (1971), *Dirty Linen and Newfoundland* (1976), *Dogg's Hamlet and Cahoot's Macbeth* (1979).

After Magritte is, like *Rosencrantz,* indicative of some crucial distinctions between Stoppard and the absurdists.

The play presents several characters who act in ostensibly absurd patterns: Harris, for instance, is apparently trying to blow out an electric light as the play opens; Thelma seems to be crawling around the room desultorily. Mother lies on an ironing board with a derby perched on her stomach. This opening tableau evinces the fact that Magritte is Stoppard's favorite artist and that Stoppard's plays have obvious affinities with the surrealists. But the crucial distinction between the surrealists and Stoppard (and perhaps between Magritte and Stoppard) lies in the fact that even in this dramatic microcosm rationality still prevails. The opening tableau has only the appearance of surrealism; it is bizarre, even foolish—but it is not surreal. All of the characters have explanations or at least rationalizations for their behavior that is not random but based on causality just as surely and as delicately as the light fixture and fruit basket balance by each other. Logic prevails as it turns out that Reginald is not trying to extinguish the electric light but is blowing on the bulb in order to cool it. Similarly, Thelma is crawling around on the floor to find her lost earring. However unorthodox and meaningless their actions seem, they are motivated and reasoned. Like everything that Stoppard has written, *After Magritte* and its situations have reasonable explanations. The activities and perceptions of Stoppard's characters are often extraordinary, but always predicated on the character's version or perversion of rationality.

The principal ironies of the plot revolve around the fact that rather than playing out absurd roles or behaving in unmotivated ways, Mother, Reginald, and Thelma are creatures who completely rely on logic and causality. "There is," as Reginald remarks, "a perfectly logical reason for everything."[11] Moreover, the Magritte exhibition that the Harris family attended at the Tate Gallery was unsatisfactory to Mother, despite a penchant shared by her and Magritte for the tuba; Thelma found Magritte's paintings disappointing: "not from life you know?" (p. 30).

Like *Jumpers* and *The Real Inspector Hound*, *After Magritte* parodies the logical legerdemain associated with British crime detection since the days of Arthur Conan

11. Stoppard, *After Magritte* (London: Faber, 1969), p. 32.

Doyle. Although little action occurs in the course of the play, the characters recount for each other and then for Inspector Foot an episode they observed on Ponsonby Place after leaving the Magritte exhibition at the Tate Gallery. Mother saw a man "playing hopscotch on the corner, a man in a loose-fitted striped gaberdine of a convicted felon. He carried a handbag under one arm and with the other he waved at me with a cricket bat. . . . wearing dark glasses, and a surgical mask" (pp. 38–39). Reginald argues that the handbag was tortoise (one of Stoppard's favorite animals); the hopscotch was not child's game at all, but rather the hobbling of a one-legged man; the cricket bat was his cane; the surgical mask a beard; and the dark glasses further proof of his blindness. Thelma has yet another set of explanations for the episode: the man's shirt was that of a West Bromwich Albion footballer; he carried a football (or perhaps a wineskin, a bagpipe, or a yashmak) and an ivory cane and had shaving cream on his face.

But the truth of the matter comes in darkness—a temporary blackout caused by the exchange of light bulbs—from Inspector Foot. The man, it turns out, whom the Harrises saw was none other than Foot himself. While shaving in his home on Ponsonby Place, Foot notice a parking space freed by the Harrises' departure. Wanting to set a good example for his fellow police officers, Foot dashed out of his home, grabbing his wife's pocketbook for change for the meter, and an umbrella as protection against the rain, but inadvertently jammed both his legs into one leg of his pajama. A migraine prompted him to wear dark glasses.

The final tableau of the play is at least as improbable as its opening scene, but the audience is now gifted with understanding. As rational creatures, the audience is satisfied and delighted to find the final tableau entirely intelligible. Reginald sports green rubber waders to avoid an electrical shock from the poorly wired light fixtures; he dons his wife's evening gown in order for her to take up its hem; he wears evening dress trousers for his "professional engagement at the North Circular Dancerama" (p. 36). Chief Inspector Foot, whose ridiculous hasty dash to the meter occasioned all the confusion among the Harris family, who prides himself on his strict adherence to methodical analysis and logic, in fact behaves even more ludicrously than Reginald, Thelma, or Mother.

The greatest irony of *After Magritte* is based, Stoppard has said, on an actual incident.

> It was based on fact for a start—somebody I know had a couple of peacocks in the garden, and one escaped while he was shaving. He chased it and he had to cross a main road to catch it, and he was standing in his pyjamas with shaving cream on his face holding a peacock when the traffic started going by.
>
> ("Ambushes," p. 17)

Whereas the ultimate explanations for the bizarre tableaux struck at the beginning and end of *After Magritte* are both improbable and implausible, they are certainly not impossible. Indeed, by the play's end they seem downright sensible and even a trifle common. As Reginald says: "The activities in this room have been broadly speaking of a mundane nature" (p. 44).

Herein lies not only the confirmation of his assertion that there are logical explanations for everything but also another crucial distinction between Stoppard and the surrealists as well as the absurdists. Whereas Magritte's paintings illustrate the fragmentary and incomprehensible nature of contemporary man's existence, Stoppard's plays demonstrate the possibility of dealing logically with an ostensibly disordered world. It seems altogether likely that Magritte's appeal to Stoppard grows out of the challenge that the painter's works present to the playwright's imagination: what possible sequence of events could produce the strange juxtaposition of a tuba, bowler hat, and an apple? What convoluted yet logical solution can explain their unlikely combination? Rather than accepting the surrealistic premises of Magritte's work, Stoppard retains his foothold in logic and pursues rational and even commonplace solutions while embracing the technique of the unlikely juxtaposition.

After Magritte is an appropriately ambiguous title for Stoppard's play because it simultaneously suggests that the play self-consciously fashions the tableaux after the images and patterns of Magritte's paintings, but also because it implies that the play is written in response to and perhaps even as a reaction against surrealism: As Wendell V. Harris (ironically the author of an essay about Stoppard's fictional Harris family) observes:

> But more is imported from Magritte than the tuba, and the "after" of the title carries the meaning of "in imitation of" as well as "subsequent in time to," for the opening scene is almost certainly modeled on Magritte's "L'assassin menacé."[12]

Whereas Stoppard obviously exploits the style of Magritte's paintings in the opening and closing scenes of his play, he borrows little of Magritte's surrealistic substance—little, that is, of the enthusiasm for the liberation of the unconscious. Logic, not the unconscious, is vindicated and celebrated by *After Magritte*.

Stoppard's fondness for Magritte seems unlikely, but he has overcome the typical interpretation of Magritte's work by adding an entirely new plane of imaginative interpretation of the surrealist's paintings. Beginning with a tableau that draws upon Magritte's iconography (bowler hats, tubas), Stoppard juxtaposes objects incongruously. Hence, the elaborately described opening of *After Magritte* confronts the audience with an apparently surreal or absurdist comment on contemporary domesticity. Moreover, the dialogue that begins the play offers little hope that we are on the firm and easily identified turf of representational theatre.

After Magritte is ultimately an anti-surrealist play. Surrealists see the tangible realities as a snare that will fetter and eventually diminish both the intellect and the imagination. Through a wide variety of techniques (Dali's distorted representation of familiar objects, Magritte's naturalistic presentation of commonplace objects in incongruous arrangements, Breton's collages), the surrealists sought to liberate the imagination from the ordinary to pursue the fantastic. The anti-surrealistic quality of Stoppard's play derives from his borrowing Magritte's technique (the star-

12. Wendell V. Harris, "Stoppard's *After Magritte*," *Explicator* 34 (1976): 1926.

tling, impossible arrangement of familiar objects) but rather than provoking the surreal or fantastic, *After Magritte* pursues logical conclusions. Whereas Magritte took the mundane as his starting point for his fantasy, Stoppard begins with the fantastic and then demonstrates its commonness. Essentially Stoppard has, even in his work in the sixties, favored the real world (that of the commonplace, logic, and, at least, the possibility of knowing) over the world of fantasy. That choice anticipates his increasing concern with substantive issues in the late seventies as well as his unflattering portrayal of the avant-gardist Beauchamp in *Artist Descending a Staircase.*

Leonard Goldstein views *After Magritte* as a refutation of the existentialists, as well as Stoppard's own *Rosencrantz and Guildenstern*: "Stoppard's little play reasserts the knowability of the world through reason as against the Surrealists, the Existentialists, the Absurdists, and some philosophically-minded scientists."[13] Although Goldstein does not discuss *After Magritte*'s relationship to *Rosencrantz and Guildenstern,* we are left to infer that the absurdist elements of the latter are refuted by the former.

Although Stoppard is consistently more discursive than most of the absurdists, *After Magritte,* as well as *The Real Inspector Hound,* offers a plausible connection with Beckett and Ionesco in its treatment of language. As for the absurdists, the comedy of *After Magritte* grows out of lexical misunderstandings, puns, and a keen sense of the limitations of language to communicate. Hence, René Magritte is confused with George Simenon's fictional police detective Maigret; ivory canes are mistaken for the white sticks used by the blind ("An ivory cane IS a white stick" [p. 19]). When Foot suggests that the pile of furniture blocking the front door indicates that the Harrises *were* expecting visitors, Thelma can reply: "I am prepared to defend myself against any logician you care to produce" (p. 30). Language compounds rather than resolves the confusion and misunderstandings about the events that transpired on Ponsonby Place. As Inspector Foot grills his suspects on their experience at the scene of the alleged crimes, he tries

13. Leonard Goldstein, "A Note on Tom Stoppard's *After Magritte,*" *Zeitschrift fur Anglistik und Amerikanstik* 23 (1975): 21.

desperately to seek out logical flaws and inconsistencies; he is, of course, wonderfully successful because the accounts vary so radically. Unconsciously, Thelma points out the limitations if not futility of language in her ironic statement "there's no need to use language"—the only line repeated verbatim in the course of the play (pp. 11, 15). Indeed, language confounds and convolutes the otherwise readily intelligible situation of *After Magritte*. According to Crossley:

> The end of the play is another version of the opening pose. Thus, there is a deliberate attempt to re-create in the audience the sense of "this is where we came in." This circularity of design therefore denies in *After Magritte* the sense of an ending.
>
> (p. 84)

Although the final tableau certainly does recall the opening scene, the crucial difference between them lies in the audience's understanding. The play has indeed come full circle, but by the final scene the audience, as armchair detective, has solved the case. What appeared as an absurd, bizarre spectacle has been transformed into an intelligible scene of domestic activity. Constable Holmes (the inept shadow of his namesake) "recoils into paralysis" (p. 47) at the final tableau only because he has been elsewhere occupied in obtaining a search warrant. Although the audience may feel that this is where they first came in, they also experience the satisfaction of grasping an entirely logical explanation, a satisfaction not at all unlike that provided by the conclusion to a whodunnit. A similar structural repetition occurs both at the beginning of *Jumpers* and in its Coda. In each instance, the central acrobat in a human pyramid is murdered, literally blown away, and the pyramid collapses. But as in *After Magritte*, the Coda to *Jumpers* is accessible to the audience because it understands that McFee and Clegthorpe were murdered for the same reason and, in all probability, by the same person.

Rosencrantz, Hound, and Magritte all illustrate Stoppard's penchant and talent for architectonic balance. The elaborate patterns of doubling in *Rosencrantz*, the intricate transgression and manipulation of the fourth wall that enables Moon and Birdboot to exchange places with Simon and Puckeridge, and the parallel opening and closing tableaux of *Magritte* admirably demonstrate his ability to impose order and sense of completion on his works. More importantly, these structural devices evince the often astounding, even magical, ease with which Stoppard delights his audience. That delight, only one component of his theatricalism, diverts the audience from his more substantive themes, such as his concern with language. That delight also undercuts whatever sense of futility is implicit in the lives of Ros and Guil, Birdboot and Moon, and even Inspector Foot.

Stoppard's accomplishment during the late sixties lies in the development of a distinctive, albeit highly derivative, dramatic style. The title of Tynan's piece on Stoppard comes from a line uttered by Lord Malquist: "Since we cannot hope for order, let us withdraw with style from the chaos." In the late sixties, Stoppard's highly theatrical style evolved from his conscious exploration of what is generally thought to be the greatest work of dramatic literature and the parody of the most popular dramatic genres. Henceforth, his characters will be more fully developed as well as more original; his thematic concerns will move into the area of morality—first on the abstract level of philosophical speculation, then on the plane of aesthetics, and finally in the realm of the ethics of journalistic practices and political oppression.

IV

The opening of Stoppard's *Jumpers* can be seen as emblematic of his dramaturgy. As the unidentified, offstage voice of Sir Archibald Jumper announces Dorothy Moore, the evocation of the Music Hall Chairman is unmistakable. His speech is filled with the platitudes of enthusiasm ("the much-missed, much-loved star of the musical stage, the incomparable, magnetic Dorothy Moore")[1] that quickly drift into parody ("the incomparable, unreliable, neurotic Dorothy Moore" [p. 17]). The theatricalism, with all its attendant clichés of excitement and gaiety, is obvious but overshadowed by the next entrance: that of a secretary "on a swing, making an arc from wing to wing, in sight for a second, out of sight for a second... Each time she reappears she has taken off some clothing" (p. 17). But at this point all voyeuristic delights are frustrated by Crouch, a servant who blocks the audience's view of the ecdysiast's display. And so while the audience pleads for Crouch to step aside ("Let the dog see the rabbit!" [p. 18]), their frustration grows, culminating only as Crouch "backs into the path of the swing and is knocked arse over tip by a naked lady" (p. 18).

As playwright, Stoppard is simultaneously both the servant and the stripping secretary. Each of his plays suggests that he considers theatrical stunts, such as a stripper on a trapeze, and stock characters, such as the butler from a whodunnit, neither beneath nor beyond him. In the collision of the two, we can see the metaphoric collision of the two impulses that coexist in Stoppard's plays: pizzazz and profundity. The impulse to entertain, to dazzle, and to captivate balances the impulse to suggest that something more profound is indeed happening, to imply that our perspective may inhibit us from seeing things as they truly are, to assert that the consequential is being revealed. The audience's vision of precisely what is revealed is obscured. The audience's interest is stimulated, its imagination piqued, but if its members expect to see truth revealed, they face inevitable disappointment. While

---

1. Stoppard, *Jumpers* (New York: Grove, 1972), p. 17.

Renaissance playwrights labored under the assumption that drama must both instruct and delight, Stoppard assumes that drama might instruct but first it must delight.

Through the first decade of his career, Stoppard's own views of the debates undertaken in his plays may well have been uncertain. But, if only because of the growing number of plays he has written, his own sympathies have become increasingly evident. In the seventies, Stoppard became reticent about directly commenting on his work. As his plays have become more political, he has said less about them. His commercial success and critical acclaim obviated the need for him to publicize his plays through interviews. The interview with Stoppard that appeared in the program of the National Theatre's premiere production of *Jumpers* is indicative of his disdain for self-analysis and self-explanation. When the interviewer queried: "Bearing in mind that this is an interview to go in the programme, is there anything you would like to say about *Jumpers*?" Stoppard laconically replied, "Not really."[2]

The bizarre confusion with which *Jumpers* begins not only recalls the opening tableau of *After Magritte* but also anticipates the mayhem that envelops this work. But as disparate and fragmentary as the various events surrounding *Jumpers* may seem, there is a strong structural unity among them: all refute George Moore's intuitional faith in the deity and human altruism. The victory of the Radical Liberal political party, led by Sir Archibald Jumper, is the political disturbance that mirrors the lamentable de-mythologizing of the moon as symbolized both in Astronaut Oates's abandonment of his crew member on the moon and in Dorothy Moore's inability to remember the words to her romantic moon songs. These are the days when the worst people—the most aggressive, selfish, and materialistic—have risen to power. Similarly, other earthly events scoff and mock religious faith and faith in man. The former Secretary of Agriculture, Sam Clegthorpe, has become Archbishop of Canterbury (an appointment that is at least somewhat disappointing to him in that he was hoping for a secular, that is, more prestigious, cabinet post).

2. "Interview with Tom Stoppard," Programme for the National Theatre production of *Jumpers*, N.D., N. P.

Among the professorships, the chairs at the university, that of Logic, which is the most objective and clinical and the least human, is the most highly valued. The Chair of Divinity, the most dependent upon subjective faith and individual belief in what cannot be empirically verified, is the least prized. (George Moore's Chair of Moral Philosophy falls somewhere between the two.)

In the midst of this confusion is George Moore: to paraphrase Oscar Wilde in *The Importance of Being Earnest*, not that George Moore, but the other one. This is not George Edward Moore, born 1873, who was once one of the leading British realists and a Professor of Mental Philosophy and Logic at Cambridge. This is George Moore, Professor of Moral Philosophy at an unnamed university, author of the unfinished study *The Concept of Knowledge*. As the husband of the celebrated Dorothy Moore (not that Dorothy Moore, the other one), George stands on the fringe of theatrical society.

In his lectures to an imaginary fourth wall, George identifies this time as:

> The high point of scientism; from here on the Darwinian revolution declines to its own origins. Man has gone ape and God is in the ascendant, and it will end as it began, with him gazing speculatively down on the unpeopled earth as the moon rises over the smoking landscape of the vulcanite cliffs and lakes of clinker—not another Herculaneum, but the ash itself.
>
> (p. 39)

Indeed, by the end of the play we discover that certain events suggest that the metaphoric gyres have begun to turn already; and this is why the death of Professor Duncan McFee is central to the play, just as McFee was central to the human pyramid that his philosophy department constructed in the play's opening moments.

McFee, the murdered jumper whose corpse occasionally is seen hanging from a door in Dorothy Moore's bedroom, was to have been George Moore's opponent in the annual philosophy symposium. McFee, who was secretly engaged to Moore's disrobing secretary and who held the Chair of Logic at the university, had recently developed grave doubts about the philosophy that earned him the senior chair in his department. He had planned, as Crouch the obliging all-knowing butler tells us, to enter a monastery as a refuge against the horror of men killing one another on the moon and the confusion of modern life in general (p. 80). Like Dotty but very much unlike George, McFee took his philosophy to heart; what he believed in on an abstract plane he sought to live out on a mundane level—hence, his disillusionment with previously held philosophical convictions; hence, too, his murder.

Dotty, despite the fact that she is the prime suspect in McFee's murder, had no reason and little of the sadistic temperament or disregard for human life necessary to kill him. The principal evidence against her is her mental imbalance. In fact, virtually everyone else in the play (George, Archie, and the secretary, and the other jumpers) had stronger motives for killing McFee than did Dorothy. George has at least the motive of professional jealousy although little of the requisite malice or amorality. The secretary, one might presume, has abandonment and unrequited love as potential inspiration. But Archibald Jumper clearly has both the motive and the moral insensitivity to murder McFee. From the moment of his first appearance on stage, Archie evidently knows of McFee's death since he knows that the Chair of Logic is now vacant. After haggling with Inspector Bones over an appointment to the university faculty much in the same spirit that a street merchant might dicker over the price of his goods, Archie finally offers Bones the Chair of Logic (p. 65). Archie, therefore, not only knows of the vacancy but also of the need to divert Bones's investigation. He also admits that he and McFee "had a furious row last night" (p. 68). Moreover, Dotty believes that Archie killed McFee (p. 78). But most importantly, McFee's conversion would have proved embarrassing and possibly even disastrous to Archie as he desperately needed a spokesman at the annual symposium.

There is a flimsy thread of allusion to Shakespeare's *Macbeth* running throughout *Jumpers*. The first clue to this parallel comes when Dotty, responding to McFee's death, calls out "Oh horror, horror, horror!" (p. 24). Those are, of course, Macduff's lines from *Macbeth* upon the discovery of the king's murder (2.3.63, 66–67). Moreover, McFee

61

shares with the murdered king not only a Scottish ancestry (Archie says he and McFee argued because he called Edinburgh "the Reykjavik of the South" [p. 68]), but also the name Duncan.[3] (The mining of Shakespeare is also found in one of George's asides to his tortoise: "Now might I do it, Pat" [p. 43], which is a newly punctuated theft of Hamlet's contemplation of Claudius at prayer: "Now might I do it Pat, now he is praying" [3.3.73]).

One of Stoppard's favorite ways of manipulating logic and simultaneously inciting dramatic action is to make the figurative the literal. No play provides a better example of this technique than *Jumpers*. The play's themes, all of which seem to hover about the periphery of its chaotic action, reinforce this pattern of making the figurative literal. Because George Moore is a moral philosopher who depends upon supporting his arguments by drawing examples from tangible areas of human experience, Stoppard fills his study with ludicrously real objects intended to demonstrate metaphoric truths. George stalks his study armed with bow and arrow to illustrate Zeno's paradox that before an arrow can reach its target it must first cover half the distance and then half the remaining distance, and so on. His pets include a hare, Thumper, and a tortoise, Pat, should he need to illustrate the virtues of perseverance over self-confidence and native ability. (The great irony here is that the literalization of these metaphors is almost certain to belie whatever figurative truth they contain.) But the literalization of the figurative is not confined to George; it is a structural pattern that touches all of the play's characters. For Dotty, this pattern appears in her failure to remember the lyrics to moon songs. With the landing of the British astronauts on the moon and the televised proof of their selfishness, the moon has been demythologized. What was once a symbol of love, desire, the unattainable, and the willing suspension of reason is now just an identifiable landscape where the meanness of man is equally as apparent as on the earth's surface. In her final line of the play, Dotty laments the loss of the moon's romantic and

3. In "Historical Homonyms: A New Way of Naming in Tom Stoppard's *Jumpers*," *Modern Drama* 22 (1979): 307, Mary R. Davidson points out that McFee literally means "son of faith."

imaginative powers: "Goodbye, spoony, Juney moon" (p. 89).

The title of the play as well as many of the puns about mental gymnastics and leaps of faith also exploit this technique of literalizing the figurative. When asked for the National Theatre program if the play was actually about people jumping, Stoppard replied, "definitely." (The program at the National Theatre was filled with photographs of J. Robert Oppenheimer, Aldous Huxley, and Paul Tillich jumping.) One of the givens of *Jumpers* is that a philosophy department literally engages in the physical acrobatics that normally would be confined to the metaphysical plane. Those gymnastics come at the behest of the Vice-Chancellor of the university whose main interest is the trampoline (p. 61).

The literalization of the figurative is also related to and perhaps an extension of the relationship between life and art and between life and acting—questions that Stoppard had earlier explored, notably in *Rosencrantz and Guildenstern.* The strongest link between literalizing the figurative and playacting in *Jumpers* is George's interpretation of Dotty's actions as clues in a running game of charades. Once Dotty has drawn George away from the composition of his lecture with cries of "Help! Murder! . . . Rape! . . . Wolves! . . . Fire!" (pp. 24–28), she implores him to stay with her, to play games with her. When he finds her nude body sprawled lifelessly across the bed, he quickly determines that she is a book, *The Naked and the Dead* (p. 30).

The rift between life and art, between life and playacting also bears upon the question of George's life and his philosophy. As in previous plays, especially *The Real Inspector Hound,* language is in no small part responsible for the difference between what characters say and what they do. But whereas Birdboot and Moon seem to have lost control over their public, critical pronouncements but not all of their conversational speech, George has permanently lapsed into academic jargon. Bigsby asserts that "even the language which he uses subverts his intention, since it too is relativistic, a pragmatic approximation" (p. 20), but there is actually less of the pragmatic in George's language than might seem obvious at first. His intimate conversations with his neurotic wife are marked by the same Ciceronian sentence structure, tangential clauses, and rambling allusions that plague his philosophical ruminations. His speech is only one measure of the self-control that he has lost by hopelessly confusing reality and philosophical speculation. In so doing, he has fled the real world, abandoned Dotty, overlooked his observation of everyday life, and left common sense behind. As Dotty reminds him:

> You were still comparing knowledge in the sense of having-experience-of, with knowledge in the sense of being-acquainted-with, and knowledge in the sense of inferring facts with knowledge in the sense of comprehending truths, and all the time as you got more and more acquainted with, though no more comprehending of, the symbolic patterns on my Persian carpet, it was knowing in the biblical sense of screwing that you were learning about.
>
> (p. 36)

At one point, George says that "language is a finite instrument crudely applied to an infinity of ideas" (p. 62), but too often his own use of language makes it a crude instrument applied to finite ideas.

One of the central arguments of Dotty and George concerns which of them is closer to reality. George argues that Dotty, a former student of his, knows nothing of his work; he tells her, "You are the wife of an academic: that means you are twice removed from the center of events" (p. 36). Dotty, on the other hand, asserts that by ignoring all of the daily realities that surround him, from her own mental instability to the political victory of the Radical Liberals, George is "living in dreamland" (p. 31). Similarly, most everyone in the play is remarkably uninterested in what he is theoretically paid to do or at least is primarily concerned with something else. When Inspector Bones expresses a lack of interest in George's moral philosophy, he explains that "show business is my main interest, closely followed by crime detection" (p. 46). Sir Archie is more concerned with the political victory of the Radical Liberals, the trampoline, and the seduction of Dotty than with matters traditionally associated with the Vice-Chancellor of a university. McFee, the assassinated jumper, has undergone a conversion and planned to enter a monastery on the off-chance that altruism is indeed possible. Dotty, a musical-comedy singer by profession, has forgotten the words to her songs. George is oblivious to the moral vacuity of his own life. Sam Clegthorpe, the Radical Liberal spokesman for agriculture, has been appointed Archbishop of Canterbury. In short, nothing is as it was or even as it is supposed to be; no one is either what he purports to be or should be. But that there is a dystopian vision underpinning *Jumpers* is perhaps even too obvious to note. Stoppard has taken the notion that things are getting worse as a cliché and compounded the ensuing disorder to a ludicrous degree. And whereas George believes that things have become as bad as they possibly can, Dotty is less optimistic in directing her anger against technology and its lunar conquest:

> They thought it [the cause of her pre-mature retirement] was overwork or alcohol, but it was just those little grey men in goldfish bowls, clumping about in their lead boots on the television news; it was very interesting, but it certainly spoiled that Juney old moon; and much else besides.
>
> (p. 39)

George's approach to this disorder, his explanation for it, relates it directly to the current state of philosophy.

The philosophical content of *Jumpers* has been the source of considerable discussion among philosophers. Sir Alfred J. Ayer, Wykeham Professor of Logic at Oxford University and, some have suggested, a model for the play's characters, has written about *Jumpers* in the London *Sunday Times*. Two articles in the prestigious journal, *Philosophy*, were devoted to the play. Jonathan Bennett, who considers the philosophy voiced in the play irrelevant, thin, insubstantial, and boring, argues that "*Jumpers* is a poor effort which doesn't deserve its current success."[4] Bennett's rebutter, Henning Jensen, cogently argues that "there is an abundance of internal evidence to show that the author [Stoppard] shares Bennett's evaluation of these materials";[5] that is, that Stoppard himself would agree that

4. Jonathan Bennett, "Philosophy and Mr. Stoppard," *Philosophy* 50 (1975): 5.

5. Henning Jensen, "Jonathan Bennett and Mr. Stoppard," *Philosophy* 52 (1977): 215.

the philosophies of George Moore, Duncan McFee, and Archibald Jumper may indeed be irrelevant, thin, insubstantial, and perhaps even boring as those philosophies pertain to the world presented in *Jumpers*. Given the play's admittedly hyperbolic description of a none-too-distant future, the philosophies espoused by these academics seem to be one of the audience's and play's firmest links with reality. The world of *Jumpers* shows the hedonism, preoccupation with self, utilitarianism, logical positivism, and skepticism of what Tom Wolfe called "the Me decade"[6] taken to a logical extreme. Stoppard's technique in this regard is remarkably similar to that employed in *If You're Glad I'll Be Frank* or *Albert's Bridge*: he begins by asserting the existence and validity of an assumption that stretches logic and then pursues that assumption to its extreme. The assumption that underpins *Jumpers* is that the fashions of twentieth-century philosophical inquiry are not confined to the halls of academe or to the minds of academicians but are employed in the politics, religion, and daily life of the nonacademic world. It has become a commonplace that twentieth-century philosophy in particular and ontological studies in general have nothing to do with life as it is lived. This conclusion grows out of the extreme abstraction, highly specialized jargon, and self-reflective qualities endemic to such studies. Similar thoughts about contemporary art are often voiced. In *Jumpers*, Dorothy Moore, besieged by neuroses and disillusionments, articulates the irrelevance of philosophical speculation in general and her husband's in particular. As George Moore starts at what he identifies as the beginning with the question "is God?" Dorothy cries in panic, desperate to attract his attention.

Treated seriously, the philosophical confrontation of *Jumpers* pits the intuitionists against the rationalists; the spiritualists against the materialists. However disparaged the philosophy of the play may be by academic metaphysicians, the sad truth is that *Jumpers* depicts the principal confrontation that characterizes twentieth-century philosophy. While thinkers have undergone what the nineteenth

6. Tom Wolfe, "The Third Great Awakening," *Mauve Gloves and Madmen, Clutter and Vine* (New York: Farrar, Straus, & Giroux, 1967), p. 126.

century sometimes called the dark night of the soul for most of the recorded history of philosophy, the twentieth century's philosophical thought pivots on the very question of the possibility of faith or belief in something outside the individual.

Fragments of George's philosophy are littered throughout the play; they are given marginal coherence in the lecture George is composing for the annual symposium. Perhaps the most reasonable and accessible statement of George's position comes after an angry outburst at Dotty in an aside to Pat the tortoise:

> The irrational, the emotional, the whimsical . . . these are the stamp of humanity which makes reason a civilizing force. In a wholy [sic] rational society the moralist will be a variety of crank, haranguing the bus queue with the demented certitude of one blessed with privileged information—"Good and evil are metaphysical absolutes!"
>
> (p. 40)

This is, of course, a statement of the intuitionists' belief that is so baldly straightforward and succinct that it surely would attract few academic subscribers. Herein lies the greatest obstacle that Stoppard had to face in writing a dramatic work that deals with philosophy: the subject matter itself is so deeply entrenched in its own history, jargon, and cross-references that to be accessible to a theatrical audience it must be drastically simplified and, some might say, reduced to its lowest common denominator. Dramatically, Stoppard is fully cognizant of this problem and handles it by giving George and Dotty (who often serves as an unenthusiastic mouthpiece for Archie's relativism or plays devil's advocate to her husband) the most direct utterance of their respective views in a farcical and informal situation (a domestic quarrel, immediately after speaking to a turtle). In such casual and intimate circumstances, the philosophy voiced by Stoppard's characters makes more sense than in George's rambling, convoluted symposium lecture.

The ironies of this situation abound: George's moral concerns are immediately applicable to both his domestic situation and the political events of his day; he fails to appreciate this since he is thoroughly immured in his self-conscious academic pose. George is, after all, the one who has argued for the applicability of metaphysical convictions to daily life; yet Archie is the one whose life embodies his philosophical stance. Moreover, in the world of *Jumpers*, George is a "variety of crank" haranguing, in this instance, the other characters and the audience with his demented certitude.

At the heart of that position espoused by Archie appears to be the conviction that, as Dotty facetiously says: "Things and actions, you understand, can have any number of real and verifiable properties. But good and bad, better and worse, these are not real properties of things, they are just expressions of our feelings about them" (p. 41).

In the confrontation between the intuitionists and the more popular neological positivists, the two positions are represented by George's utterances in his lecture (and far less by what he actually does, for instance, in his relationship with Dotty) and by the slick, opportunistic style of Archibald Jumper. McFee, one must assume, previously could have given scholarly voice to the arguments of Jumper and the logical positivists. George's philosophical stance is best stated in his last speech (p. 88). Although George defines his beliefs principally in opposition to those of the logical positivists, his best point is that knowledge is not simply a collection of empirically verifiable facts—such as the Bristol train leaves from Paddington station—but an adventure into that dangerous region of faith and belief.

Archie's view, which can hardly be called a philosophy in spite of the liberal application of that term to George's thought, is most clearly stated in his final speech that embodies his left-handed sort of optimism ("vast areas are unpolluted; millions of children grow up without suffering deprivation, and millions, while deprived and cruelly treated, none the less grow up." [pp. 88–89]). Life will go on, Archie suggests, and so the best possible course of action seems to be to make it as comfortable and easy as possible.

The Coda to *Jumpers*, structurally the weakest and the most confusing part of the play, is the philosophical symposium "in bizarre dream form" (p. 83). More specifically, the Coda gives the audience George's dream of what transpires at the debate. George, for instance, refuses to question Captain Scott, asking, "Why should I cross-examine the figures of my dreams?" (p. 85).

Basically, the action of the Coda reiterates the action of the first act insofar as the new Archbishop of Canterbury follows the pattern established by McFee. Both Clegthorpe and McFee were thoroughgoing materialists who received their respective appointments to the church and university hierarchies because, in essence, they demonstrated an ability and willingness "to jump"—to serve as figureheads and mouthpieces. Both, however, experienced a crisis of disbelief that led them to doubt the philosophies they were presumed to represent; both came, in other words, to believe at least in the possibility of altruism, transcendent values, and absolutes. The conversion or crucial skepticism of McFee and Clegthorpe brought those who originally appointed them to the conclusion that they were too embarrassing to tolerate and, hence, would have to be eliminated.

In the Coda, this confrontation centers on Clegthorpe's assertion that "surely belief in man could find room for man's belief?" (p. 86). When Clegthorpe presses his point, noting that he *is* the Archbishop of Canterbury, Archie paraphrases Henry II's famous line about Thomas à Becket: "*Will no one rid me of this turbulent priest!*" (p. 86). That one statement sets the jumpers jumping, leaping about the stage in a choreography that will serve as a dance of death for Clegthorpe. In this instance, Archie's responsibility for the murder seems much clearer than in the case of McFee. Like McFee, his philosophical counterpart, Clegthorpe is framed by a troupe of acrobats in a pyramid that disintegrates as its keystone is blown away by a gunshot blast. Bigsby summarizes this action by emphasizing George's complicity:

> Though himself an atheist, he proceeds to imitate Thomas Becket and voices the opinion, heretical in a rational state, that "surely belief in man could find room for man's beliefs." When he is consequently murdered for this affront to ration-

ality and political expediency, George fails to intervene, unwilling to make the necessary connection between theory
and practice.

(p. 21)

Kenneth Tynan has no doubt as to Stoppard's own position:

> In that great debate there is no question where Stoppard
> stands. He votes for the spirit—although he did not state his
> position in the first person until June of this year [1977],
> when, in the course of a book review, he defined himself as a
> supporter of "Western liberal democracy, favouring an in-
> tellectual elite and a progressive middle class and based on a
> moral order derived from Christian absolutes."

(p. 96)

That Stoppard's personal philosophy probably has much
more in common with George's than with Archie's confirms his statements about his dramatic strategy. Certainly,
he has not idealized George as the spokesman of the truth.
George is everything Archie is not. Superficially, Archie is
a success (an entertainer of celebrities, a cohort of political
victors, a gadabout of great panache), while George is a
failure (hopelessly disorganized, maritally betrayed,
philosophically passé). But if Archie is a success, he is one
only in the most worldly and materialistic of terms; and,
conversely, if George is a failure, he is one only because he
fails to carry through in his beliefs, to enact the philosophy
he enunciates.

Artist Descending a Staircase takes up an issue that is
present only in embryonic form in *Jumpers* but which is
central to *Travesties, Night and Day,* and *Cahoot's Macbeth*:
the responsibility of an individual to his society, his
friends, and himself. As in *Travesties* and *Cahoot's Macbeth*,
the question of the artist's responsibility is scrutinized in
detail. Like many of his protagonists, Stoppard, at least in
his previous work, shied away from full engagement in the
world, preferring instead the relative comfort and security
that comes with donning an artistic persona glazed with
cynicism. *Artist Descending a Staircase* marks a turning point
in Stoppard's career in that, first, the problem he considers

here is more specialized than those of his previous plays, and, second, a wide variety of clues (ranging from his own statements to the particular tone of this play) suggests he is moving toward firm commitment, toward certain beliefs. The more specific the thematic focus of Stoppard's plays is, the more clearly we can see genuine concern for that issue. Whereas Stoppard is relatively more detached in earlier works such as *Enter a Free Man* and *Rosencrantz and Guildenstern* (despite their universal themes such as man's inability to communicate, his futility, his illusions, and self-deceptions), he is far more involved in the later plays with their focused treatment of problems like the communist repression of actors, the sad state of journalism, or the responsibility of the artist. If Stoppard seeks to bring about the successful union of farce and the play of ideas, the emphasis in the plays up to *Artist Descending a Staircase* has been on the techniques of the former while those that follow stress the content of the latter.

Artist Descending a Staircase, written and first produced in the same year as *Jumpers,* is Stoppard's most ambitious and complex work for radio. Structurally, it is arranged in a palindromic series of flashbacks and flash forwards; beginning in the present, the play moves back a couple of hours, then to last week, then leaps to 1922, 1920, and finally 1914. In the reverse order, the sequence then returns the action to the present. For the original broadcast by the BBC Radio, two sets of actors were used to play the younger (1914–1922) and older (the "here and now") characters so that the play's chronology would be clear to a listening audience.

The fact that Stoppard chose artists (although admittedly not writers) for his characters in this play indicates that he is considering the meaning and validity of his own work through drama. Not since the drama critics appeared of *The Real Inspector Hound* has a direct link existed between Stoppard and his characters; even in that instance, he showed greater interest in parody than in serious self-appraisal. (By the time Stoppard wrote *Hound* he was no longer a drama critic; when he wrote *Artist,* he was an artist writing about artists.) The same detachment tinged with cynicism that can clearly be seen in Stoppard's work also appears in at least two of the three artists as they appear in the middle of this play; that is, as they were as young men in the 1914 episode. Beauchamp, perhaps acknowledging Stoppard's own self-consciousness, says: "How can the artist justify himself? The answer is that he cannot, and should stop boring people with his egocentric need to try."[7] Martello's cynicism about the imminent world war surfaces in his observation that "those Middle Europeans are always assassinating each other" (p. 106). Donner, however, is distinctly fretful as he walks through France in 1914; he is not only physically uncomfortable, but far less adventuresome than either of his companions. By 1920, Donner is smitten by the charms of Sophie, and within two years, by the time of her suicide, he has abandoned all detachment and fallen in love with her. As an older man, Donner, the artist who has literally descended the staircase as the play opens, has grown even more cantankerous and quarrelsome. For decades he has sought to preserve the memory of Sophie in various artistic media while coming to despise Beauchamp not only for his careless and casual treatment of Sophie but also for his style in art.

The names and works of the three artists suggest a pastiche of styles and ideas gleaned from the history of twentieth-century art. Martello's name invokes, of course, James Joyce's tower in *Ulysses,* but the image goes no further except that Joyce himself appears as a character in *Travesties,* which is in various ways indebted to *Artist.* Beauchamp's name, as it is spelled (though not as it is pronounced, Beech-um) conjures up Marcel Duchamp, an allusion reinforced by the play's title and Duchamp's most celebrated painting "Nude Descending a Staircase." But Beauchamp has long since abandoned painting: even in 1920, while toying with recorded sounds, he sought "to liberate the visual *image* from the limitations of visual *art*" (p. 98). This tautology alone suggests the superficiality of Beauchamp's work as well as his thinking. Even as a young man in 1920, Beauchamp's justification for and explanation of his art is more important than the art itself. He is, at least in this way, one of the first conceptual artists. From the

7. Stoppard, "Artist Descending a Staircase," in *Albert's Bridge,* p. 105.

recorded table-tennis games between celebrities of the day, Beauchamp pursued the direction of the minimalists by first removing the visual image, then the celebrities, and finally even the Ping-Pong. He hopes that eventually he can eliminate everything to produce his "masterwork of accumulated silence" (pp. 78–79).

Donner, who is in one way or another Beauchamp's rival and adversary throughout the play, has become something of an aesthetic reactionary in old age. As he tells Beauchamp:

> I very much enjoyed my years in that child's garden of easy victories known as the avant garde, but I am now engaged in the infinitely more difficult task of painting what the eye sees.
>
> (p. 81)

After some experiments with "ceramic bread and steak and strawberries with plaster-of-paris cream" (p. 87) (suggesting the works of Claus Oldenberg), Donner has not only returned to representational art, but has taken up portraiture. That decision, scorned by Beauchamp, was predicated on Donner's devotion to Sophie and his desire to preserve her beauty as accurately as possible.

While Beauchamp emerges as the fool who is oblivious of beauty, love, art, and virtually everything else to which a true artist should be particularly sensitive, and Donner returns to the most conventional sort of painting, Martello provides a third alternative. His cynicism is the most thoroughgoing among the three and, when combined with his perceptive intelligence, leads him to the conclusion that:

> I have achieved nothing with my life!—my brain is on a flying trapeze that outstrips all the possibilities of action. Mental acrobatics, Beauchamp—I have achieved nothing but mental acrobatics—*nothing*!
>
> (p. 78)

Given the fact that *Artist* was written the same year that *Jumpers* (which employs mental acrobatics as its central metaphor) was produced, it is likely that Martello's idea of his work might well have occurred to Stoppard about his own.

However serious the differences among Martello, Beauchamp, and Donner, there was a time when the three shared a common style of painting and a common temperament. Sophie recalls the time of their first exhibition, "Frontiers in Art," by remembering "you were such cards, weren't you?, all of you merry, not at all like artists but all three strapping schoolboy cricketers growing your first pale moustaches" (p. 95); ". . . you were all fair, and well built . . . all wearing your army uniforms, all identical" (p. 102). The central irony of *Artist Descending a Staircase* hinges upon just how similar their works were at that time. Sophie, who saw the exhibit and remembers exchanging looks with one (although she doesn't know which) of the three before she went blind, recalls that there was a painting " . . . a border fence in the snow" (p. 103) whose artist stood before it. From that one encounter, she singled out one of the three; as she says: "I wouldn't have called it love myself, but it seems to be the word people use for it" (p. 96). Donner eventually discovers, thanks to Martello, that it was he with whom Sophie fell in love, but it was also Donner himself who mistakenly told Sophie that the object of her affection was Beauchamp.

Martello's cynical view of art and his own failures, Beauchamp's ludicrous experiments in art, and the question of the responsibility, function, and subject of the artist link *Artist Descending a Staircase* and *Travesties*. In addition, World War I and Switzerland are settings that also appear in *Travesties*. But perhaps the most important link between the two is a definition of an artist that is first spoken by Donner and then repeated verbatim by Henry Carr: "An artist is someone who is gifted in some way which enables him to do something more or less well which can only be done badly or not at all by someone not thus gifted" (*Artist*, p. 83; *Travesties*, p. 38).

Travesties also shares with *Artist* nearly identical statements on the artist's privileged position in society; in *Artist* the sentiment is voiced by Beauchamp (p. 105) and in *Travesties* by Carr:

What is an artist? For every thousand people there's nine hundred doing the work, ninety doing well, nine doing good, and one lucky bastard who's the artist.[8]

But whereas Carr's use of this idea is part of his splenetic attack on Tzara, Beauchamp's statement is simply a confirmation of his charmed, albeit empty, life as an artist. Moreover, two characters from *Artist,* Beauchamp and Martello, are at least incidentally linked to *Travesties'*s Tristan Tzara and James Joyce. One of Beauchamp's artistic endeavors was to record on tape "a bubbling cauldron of squeaks, gurgles, crackles, and other unharmonious noises" (p. 81); similarly, as Esslin notes, on 26 May 1920 Tzara presented his Vaseline Symphonique at the Salle Gaveau, "a cacaphony of inarticulate sounds" (p. 320). The link between Martello and Joyce is less arcane—Joyce wrote part of *Ulysses* at Martello Tower in Sandycove just outside Dublin.

Just as *Jumpers* afforded Stoppard the opportunity to criticize the increasingly abstract, rarefied direction of contemporary philosophy, so he implicitly criticizes contemporary art in *Artist* and *Travesties.* Before Donner returned to traditional values, he is said to have run the gamut of modernism ("symbolism, surrealism, imagism, vorticism, fauvism, cubism—Dada, drip-action, hard-edge, pop, found objects and post-object" [p. 84]). Beauchamp's tapes of accumulated silence are analogous to the reductivism that is characteristic of contemporary painting and nicely promulgated in Ad Reinhardt's "Twelve Rules for a New Academy."[9] In *Travesties,* Stoppard pits the proponents of Dadaism, socialist realism, conventional bourgeois art, and Joycean modernism against one another.

Another striking similarity between *Jumpers* and *Travesties* has been pointed out by Stoppard himself:

You start with a prologue which is slightly strange. Then you have an interminable monologue which is rather funny.

8. Stoppard, *Travesties* (New York: Grove, 1974), p. 62.
9. See Ad Reinhardt, "Twelve Rules for a New Academy," in *The New Art,* ed. Gregory Battcock (New York: Dutton, 1973), pp. 167–70.

Then you have scenes. Then you end up with another monologue. And you have unexpected bits of music and dance, and at the same time people are playing ping-pong with various intellectual arguments.

(Hayman, p. 12)

Although similar in structure, *Travesties* never ventures into the surrealistic style that characterizes the Coda to *Jumpers*; moreover, *Travesties* also superimposes Wilde's *The Importance of Being Earnest* over its already convoluted plot.

Travesties is well named for several specific reasons. Its fictionalization of historical characters is a travesty of the individual, but that travesty is inevitably and necessarily committed whenever historical personages appear on stage. Its debates about art and artistic responsibility reduce delicate aesthetic theories to the level of name-calling, brawling invective. ("By God, you supercilious streak of Irish puke! You four-eyed, bog-ignorant potatoe-eating ponce!" [p. 62] is Tzara's way of addressing the most influential, adulated novelist of the twentieth century.) The play's action is, quite literally, the travesty of human existence, the reductio ad absurdum that found dramatic life in, among others, the plays of Oscar Wilde. Finally, its plot is a travesty, however laudatory and respectful, of Wilde's *The Importance of Being Earnest.* Stoppard's own devotion to Wilde dates back at least to when he was reviewing in Bristol. In *Travesties,* both Joyce and Carr show great respect for Wilde and for his belief that art need not be politically or socially oriented.

The principal cause of these travesties is that most of the play, with the possible exception of the first section of Act 2, is governed by the recollections of Henry Carr, who supposes himself to have been the British Consul in Zurich in 1918. Like Ros and Guil, the historic Carr (actually a minor official at the British Consulate) played a nearly insignificant role in this momentous political situation, although he did play the pivotal role of Algernon in a production of *The Importance of Being Earnest* arranged by Joyce in Zurich. He has twice been immortalized in literature: first by Joyce who portrayed him as the loathsome Private Carr of the Circe episode of *Ulysses;* and second by Stoppard's play. *Travesties* shows us Carr both as a dapper civil servant (Young Carr) and as a broken old man trying to live down the humiliation of Joyce's treatment by telling his story in his memoirs. But Carr's memory is hardly accurate; as Stoppard tells us in a stage direction:

> The [first] scene (and most of the play) is under the erratic control of Old Carr's memory, which is not notably reliable, and also of his various prejudices and delusions. One result is that the story (like a toy train perhaps) occasionally jumps the rails and has to be restarted at the point where it goes wild.
>
> (p. 27)

Travesties presents four distinct views on art through its four male principals: Lenin professes a belief in art as an instrument of the Marxist revolution; Tzara represents Dadaist anti-art; Joyce is the spokesman of art for art's sake; and Carr holds a relatively innocuous bourgeois view of art. Lenin's Marxist aesthetic is also voiced by his disciples, Cecily (his secretary and librarian), and Nadya (his wife). Interestingly, Carr echoes a number of Joyce's statements about art (and especially about Wilde) by rephrasing them in his confrontation with Cecily in Act 2.

Tzara's and Carr's respective notions about art are the obstacles to their romances with Cecily and Gwen. Whereas Tzara is at least willing to sidestep a confrontation with Gwen about the quality of Joyce's manuscript (he tells her that he is not Tzara the Dadaist, but his brother, Jack Tzara), Carr is uncompromising in his condemnation of both the politics and aesthetics of Lenin. Hence, the love interest is complicated not by the insistence upon the name Ernest, but by the demand for compatible aesthetic theories.

Of the four perspectives set forth by Lenin, Carr, Joyce, and Tzara, three are presented with considerable care and perhaps even sympathy. Tzara's Dadaism is treated fairly, but with little credibility in *Travesties.* It is, in fact, the most easily dismissed of the four theories of art presented. Tzara's attack on Joyce, for instance, does not deny the genius of Joyce's work but instead argues that the twentieth century can no longer accommodate art for art's sake:

You've turned literature into a religion and it's as dead as all the rest, it's an overripe corpse and you're cutting fancy figures at the wake. It's too late for geniuses! Now we need vandals and desecrators, simple-minded demolition men to smash centuries of baroque subtlety, to bring down the temple, and thus finally, to reconcile the shame and the necessity of being an artist!

(p. 62)

Strangely, Tzara's Dadaism functions as Lenin would have art function—as social criticism.

John Simon assumes that Stoppard presents Lenin in a more favorable light than the other characters:

But the second act, where Lenin preponderates, things get serious, in fact, downright ponderous. All London is trying to figure out why. Did Stoppard consider Lenin's humorless zeal, transposed to the stage, funny enough *objet trouvé* as is? Or is he too much of a Marxist to dare poke fun at Lenin? Or are some of his best friends, whom he wants to keep, Marxists?[10]

Simon is mistaken on at least two counts: the very notion that the audience or Stoppard finds Lenin's speeches funny is itself ludicrous; at least tacitly it implies that everything in a comedy should be humorous. Moreover, the notion that Stoppard himself is a Marxist using this play to protect and defend his own beliefs is patently ridiculous. Nothing could, in fact, be further from Stoppard's own beliefs and his dramatic techniques. Clearly, however, the structure, characterization, and dialogue of the first section of the second act—especially as they regard Lenin—are radical departures from those of the first act.

The demonstration of the failure of the Marxist aesthetic, in truth, is the principal point of the play's second act. Critically, the second act was poorly received and became something of a scapegoat for the play's shortcomings (its lengthy set speeches, its inclusion of Lenin and Nadya, and its digressiveness). Stoppard would have had little difficulty in portraying Lenin as a comically exaggerated

10. John Simon, "London Diary V: Éclat," *New York* (26 August 1974), p. 67.

character along the lines of Tzara or Joyce. That he chose, instead, to depict Lenin considerably more realistically than either Tzara or Joyce suggests that the particular travesty connected with Lenin lies outside of his portrayal—lies instead in his contradictory aesthetic statements and his eventual rejection of art. Moreover, Lenin's portrayal anticipates Stoppard's overt protest of the communist repression in *Every Good Boy Deserves Favor*, *Professional Foul*, and *Cahoot's Macbeth*.

The failure of Lenin's aesthetic theories is evident on two grounds: first, they are self-contradictory, and, second, they are contradicted by his own visceral response to art. On the first count, Lenin argues that only the communist political state can free the artist from his capitalistic shackles and thereby offer him true independence. Simultaneously he asserts that only one style of art, which came to be known as socialist realism, is acceptable or even tolerable. For the Marxist, art can have only one function; as Cecily says in voicing the Marxist line in her confrontation with Carr, "the sole duty and justification for art is social criticism" (p. 74). Lenin, in historically accurate dialogue,[11] addresses this paradox directly but fails to appreciate the implicit contradiction:

> We want to establish and we shall establish a free press, free not simply from the police, but also from capital, from careerism, and what is more, *free from bourgeois anarchist individualism*! These last words may seem paradoxical or an affront to my audience. Calm yourselves, ladies and gentlemen! Everyone is free to write and say whatever he likes, without any restrictions. But every voluntary association, including the party, is also free to expel members who use the name of the party to advocate anti-party views.
>
> (p. 85)

Surely, Lenin places the party before art, and the reason for this grows out of his personal response to art, which is not as predictable as his politics and which is the second cause of the failure of his aesthetic suggested by Stoppard's play.

11. Like many of Lenin's speeches in *Travesties,* this speech is taken from Lenin's own writings.

In Act 2, Stoppard juxtaposes Lenin's readings from letters to various party officials with Nadya's recollections of his own reaction to plays, concerts, and novels. Lenin preferred Pushkin to Mayakovski and changed his mind only after being told that Pushkin was bourgeois. He favored Chekhov's *Uncle Vanya* over Gorki's *The Lower Depths* even though he recognized Gorki's politics as acceptable and Chekhov's as inappropriate. But that he is genuinely moved by Beethoven's "Appasionata" evinces the second contradiction in Lenin's aesthetic; because art kindles in him a sense of human dignity and worth, he must restrain himself from its enjoyment. As he says:

> I don't know of anything greater than the Appasionata. Amazing, superhuman music. It always makes me feel, perhaps naively, it makes me feel proud of the miracles that human beings can perform. But I can't listen to music often. It affects my nerves, makes me want to say nice stupid things and pat the heads of those people who while living in this vile hell can create such beauty. Nowadays we can't pat heads or we'll get our hands bitten off. We've got to *hit* heads, hit them without mercy, though ideally we're against doing violence to people... Hm, one's duty is infernally hard.
>
> (p. 89)

These, Lenin's final words in *Travesties,* indicate the paradoxical nature of the Marxist philosophy of art. Even without touching upon the question of the repression and the persecution of artists who do not conform to the party line, issues that will resurface as immediate concerns in Stoppard's subsequent work, the failure of Lenin's aesthetic is self-evident—literally evident from his own response to art. Marx said that religion is the opiate of the people; Lenin seems to realize that art is dangerous for similar reasons.

The aesthetic position represented by Joyce is essentially a belief in art for art's sake. As Stoppard notes in the stage directions, the James Joyce who appears to perform magic tricks and to speak in limericks "is obviously an Irish nonsense" (p. 33). In Act 1, Joyce squares off against Tzara's Dadaism, but he is never pitted against the Marxist position or Carr's eclectic views of art. Most of the confrontation between Tzara and Joyce is little more than exposition concerning the Dadaist's perspective; Joyce's own view on art is, in fact, limited to one speech in which he describes the artist as "the magician put among men to gratify—capriciously—their urge for immortality" (p. 62). In direct antithesis to Lenin's art-as-social-criticism aesthetic, Joyce cites the Trojan War as an example in which great art was derived from suffering and death that otherwise have been relegated to widely unknown ancient history.

Joyceans were generally tolerant if not enthusiastic of the travesty of their master. Myron Schwartzman in *James Joyce Quarterly* writes: "The portrait is light, funny, and finally complimentary. Joyce through Carr's memory comes away no worse than Bloom in the eye of the 'Cyclops' narrator."[12] Others, however, assume that Joyce fares no better than Tzara or Lenin. Craig Werner argues that Joyce's position is undercut because Carr, who typifies the modern reader to whom literature must appeal, "actively rejects both Lenin (on patriotic grounds) and Joyce (for personal reasons)."[13] But Joyce's aesthetic, even his very presence, stimulates Young Carr and agitates Old Carr. The antipathy between them centers on a financial squabble over twenty-five francs for tickets to *Earnest* and the purchase of a pair of trousers. Carr, even as an old man, infamously humiliated in *Ulysses*, begrudgingly respects Joyce. Although Carr initially prefers Gilbert and Sullivan to Wilde (whom they satirized), the dispute between Carr and Joyce is primarily of a legal rather than an artistic nature.

After Joyce's key speech near the end of Act 1, the curtain speech for that act is a long monologue in which Old Carr bitterly recalls the litigation between him and Joyce that grew out of the production of *Earnest*. It ends with Carr's recollection of a frustrating and troublesome dream:

---

12. Myron Schwartzman, "Wilde about Joyce? Da! But My Hearts Belongs to Dada," *James Joyce Quarterly* 13 (1975): 123.
13. Craig Werner, "Stoppard's Critical Travesty, or Who Vindicates Whom," *Arizona Quarterly* 35 (1979): 235.

I dreamed about him, dreamed I had him in the witness box, a masterly cross-examination, case practically won, admitted it all, the whole thing, the trousers, everything, and I flung at him—"And what did you do in the Great War?" "I wrote *Ulysses*," he said. "What did you do?"

Bloody nerve.

(p. 65)

Importantly, this is Old Carr's nightmare; Joyce never actually said this—even Old Carr's erratic memory cannot recall him saying it. But his dream is the denial of both his lawsuit and his fondest self-aggrandizements; thus, it haunts Carr.

Carr, in fact, emulates Joyce as demonstrated by two parallel encounters. In the first, Joyce offers Carr the part of Algernon; in so doing he quotes Jack Worthing's famous line: "I may occasionally be a little overdressed but I make up for it by being immensely overeducated" (p. 52). Carr paraphrases this statement when, in Act 2, discussing the function of art he tells Cecily: "Wilde was indifferent to politics. He may occasionally have been a little over-dressed but he made up for it by being immensely uncommitted" (p. 74). The importance of the parallel lies not so much in Stoppard's or Carr's witty play on Wilde, but in the fact that Carr praises Wilde (and Joyce indirectly) by describing them as politically uncommitted. For both of them, politics has little place in their art. Joyce specifically states this when he says, "As an artist, naturally I attach no importance to the swings and roundabout of political history" (p. 50). Carr thereby models not only his sentence construction but also his apolitical view of art on borrowings from Wilde and Joyce.

Stoppard's dramatic technique often calls for him to diffuse the most significant statements with a vigorous stroke of physical comedy. In *Jumpers*, this ploy is illustrated by the rare succinctness and lucidity of George's statement that "if rationality were the criterion for things being allowed to exist, the world would be one gigantic field of soya beans" (p. 40) followed by a rhetorical question addressed to a pet. In *Travesties*, the technique is used after Joyce's catechistic interrogation of Tzara that addresses the function of art in society and its importance as a means to immortality. The speech culminates with Joyce bidding Tzara "Top o' the morning" (p. 63) and then pulling a rabbit out of his hat. The delight in seeing this bit of prestidigitation, coupled with the unlikeliness of Joyce's valediction, overshadows and undercuts what Joyce has just said.

Travesties, like *Jumpers*, does indeed take up serious themes although they are submerged beneath a highly wrought dramatic structure, dazzling dialogue, and historical or quasi-historical interludes. The examination of the question of God's existence in *Jumpers* and art's function in *Travesties* culminates Stoppard's attempt to bring about the perfect union of the comedy of ideas and farce. The satisfaction that comes, however, at the end of these plays rests principally in the legerdemain that Stoppard affects: the design is completed, the loose ends drawn together, the couples harmoniously paired off. Like Joyce, Stoppard stands as the magician of the piece.

However convincing Joyce's statements that art need not be political, Stoppard himself pursues distinctly more political themes in his subsequent work. There is no radical shift in his dramaturgy or convictions about art because whatever didacticism emerges in the most recent works again undercuts the legacy of Lenin by attacking the treatment of artists, intellectuals, and dissidents in communist countries.

With *Jumpers*, *Artist Descending a Staircase*, and *Travesties*, Stoppard begins to venture outside the self-contained worlds of philosophy and aesthetics. The luxurious flat of George and Dorothy Moore offers some shelter against the technological, political, and moral chaos outside their windows, just as Zurich in 1918 is an insular and insulated bastion of peace in the midst of war. But in these instances the grimmer realities of life immediately impinge on the lives of the characters: McFee is murdered in Mayfair; Sophie commits suicide; World War I is all too real to consular officials and political revolutionaries alike. In his next group of plays, the insularity of Stoppard's dramatic worlds will continue to diminish; his characters will draw nearer to engagement with the realities of war, political oppression, and injustice. Games will become less meaningful; reality—often of a political nature—will penetrate the defenses set up against life's problems.

Stoppard's plays had been drifting closer to engagement in the world of social and political realities since he opted for intelligibility and causality over surrealism and fantasy in *After Magritte*. Up to *Artist Descending a Staircase,* the balance between the comedy of manners and the play of ideas had always listed toward the former: pizzazz often overwhelmed profundity; the Wildean penchant for art for art's sake usually overshadowed the inclination to address topical, political issues. Although these plays still confront questions on an abstract rather than terrestrial level, *Jumpers, Artist Descending a Staircase,* and *Travesties* confront aesthetic and philosophical problems that anticipate the political matters developed in his most recent work.

V

In the late seventies, Stoppard again worked outside
the mainstream of Shaftsbury Avenue to hone and refine
his technique in order to accommodate his increasing
interest in political questions. His reputation as a successful dramatist took him in slightly different directions, but
only one of his plays of the late seventies was specifically
written for commercial production in the West End and on
Broadway. He also returned to writing for television with
Professional Foul.

Like his earlier characters, many of the protagonists of
these recent plays stand on the brink of momentous action,
participating in it only in a marginal way. Maddie Gotobed
is not actually drafting legislation, but she will shape its
substance; the journalists of *Night and Day* do not fight an
African war, but their coverage of it will determine how it
is fought; the academicians of *Professional Foul* are never
persecuted, but they witness the denial of basic human
freedoms. In *Night and Day*, the African home of the Carsons is hardly safe from the impending peril of civil insur-
rection; the committee room of *Dirty Linen* takes us to the
metaphoric heart of British government, within earshot of
Big Ben, the symbol of London. But in *Professional Foul,
Every Good Boy Deserves Favor*, and *Cahoot's Macbeth*, the
setting makes confrontation with political oppression inevitable. *Every Good Boy Deserves Favor* is the most obvious
example of this as it is set inside a Russian asylum where
political dissidents are incarcerated.

Stoppard's tendency to address political and social
themes, an impulse that first appears in *Artist Descending a
Staircase*, is central to four of the five plays he has written
since 1975. *Dirty Linen*, originally commissioned to cele-
brate the American Bicentennial, may well have taken root
in the Watergate scandal, but it soon was uprooted from
American soil and set in Britain. The nature of the scandal
it depicts is more characteristic of the British political scene
than the American. It has enjoyed the longest continuous
run of any of Stoppard's plays—surviving three seasons in
the West End.

Ironically, *Dirty Linen* is a nonpolitical play populated

by politicos: six members of Parliament, a Home Secretary, and Maddie Gotobed. It is the least substantial of all of Stoppard's plays, remarkable only as an example of Stoppard's superb craftsmanship at two of his favorite dramatic devices: verbal pyrotechnics and the extended monologue.

Basically the plot of *Dirty Linen* revolves around the fact that the newspapers have reported that one "lawnmower in knickers"[1] has seduced more than one hundred Members of Parliament or other government officials. This very woman, Maddie Gotobed, shows up, despite a paucity of secretarial skills, as the secretary to the Select Committee on Promiscuity in High Places. As the play opens, Maddie has already slept with five of the six M.P.'s on the committee. During the recess for the division bell, she will make it six of six. More importantly, she will persuade the committee that the private lives of government officials are their own and are of no concern to the press. The committee can then conclude that "this principle is not to be sacrificed to that Fleet Street stalking-horse masquerading as a sacred cow labelled 'The People's Right to Know'" (p. 72). In this way, *Dirty Linen* foreshadows the consideration of journalistic practices in *Night and Day*; both hark back to Stoppard's experience as a reporter.

The rest of the plays written since 1975 turn from the frivolous and farcical and address two specific matters: the responsibilities of the press and the communist repression of free speech and thought. Paralleling these thematic interests is Stoppard's increasing concern with the political and artistic situation in his native Czechoslovakia. Moreover, he has recently demonstrated at least a reluctant willingness to state his opinions straightforwardly and to discuss his work as an expression of his own views. His elusive political grounding has been so clarified by these recent plays that by 1977 one reviewer described Stoppard as "a committed dramatist with a cause to champion."[2] Two years later, one of his plays could be labeled *didactic*,[3] a term that may well be an overstatement but clearly indi-

---

1. Stoppard, *Dirty Linen and New-Found-Land*, (London: Faber, 1976), p. 20.
2. Albert E. Kalson, review of *Every Good Boy Deserves Favor*, *Educational Theatre Journal* 29 (1977): 563.
3. Anonymous, *What's On in London* (11 May 1979), p. 38.

cates the departure from his work prior to 1975. In an appearance before the National Press Club in Washington in 1979, Stoppard said:

> My plays on the whole are by no means spattered with sentences and speeches which speak for me, but *Night and Day* is, in some sense, an exception to that. And there are certain things in *Night and Day* to which I subscribe without qualification.

While the Soviet treatment of dissidents and the responsibilities of a free press may seem distinct problems, they are, in fact, opposite sides of the same coin: the former emphasizes what happens in a society in which free speech is suppressed; the latter stresses the abuses of free speech. In speaking about *Night and Day* before the National Press Club in 1979, Stoppard said:

> One of the characters, a reporter [Milne], in the play says that the whole point about having a free press is that for all its imperfections, if you have one then a society is essentially correctable and if you don't it's essentially concealed.... [The free press is] the absolute last line of defense.... A reasonable litmus test for a society in my view [is] is it a society where you can publish within the law?

Night and Day, then, is a reasonable continuation of the examination of the free speech and thought raised in *Professional Foul* and *Every Good Boy Deserves Favor*; the principal difference is that *Night and Day* considers the problem from the perspective of its existence in Britain rather than in communist countries.

Since 1975, Stoppard has included prefaces to three plays: *Every Good Boy Deserves Favor* and *Dogg's Hamlet* and *Cahoot's Macbeth*. In comparison to his previously cryptic statements on his work, these prefaces are downright Shavian. Still Stoppard's drama is very much the product of an artist interested in theatrical moments and cannot be easily linked with the work of what Tynan calls the "hairy men—heated, embattled, and socially committed playwrights, like John Osborne, John Arden, and Arnold Wesker" (p. 47). Two important conclusions are to be drawn here. First, the difference between Stoppard and those usually identified as playwrights of commitment (and Edward Bond's name clearly belongs in that group) is that Stoppard's social and political concerns are not the favorites of liberal, intellectual circles. His interests are neither fashionable nor liberal; compared to those of Bond or Wesker, Stoppard's concerns could be considered reactionary. The issues that were popular in the drama of this period—the unhappy lot of old people, the repressive nature of Western society, the plight of women, the handicapped, and minorities—are untouched in Stoppard's work. *Night and Day* provides an excellent example of a focused and detailed treatment of a problem in a surprising context. The context, of course, is an emerging African nation; the surprise is that the play does not address the racial problems but rather the journalistic practices that mold world opinion. No judgment of the validity of either Shimbu's or Mageeba's conflicting claims is even faintly implied in the play. Stoppard is primarily concerned with the way in which the non-African world evaluates the problems of mythical Kambawe, since his true subject is one step removed from the political quagmire that envelops the African situation. He shows that international judgments are made in spite of ignorance and that the task of comprehending the reality of the situation is presently handled through an intricate and unreliable journalistic system. Similarly, the repression of Soviet and Eastern European dissidents and artists was, at least in America circa 1970, doubted by many, especially those whose sympathies inclined them to see communism as a healthy alternative to the commercial excesses that capitalism allegedly engendered and perpetuated. Tom Wolfe argues that the greatest blow to the New Left was the publication of Aleksandr Solzhenitsyn's work because it left no doubt as to the extreme tactics that the Soviets employed to suppress free expression (pp. 122–24). But even Solzhenitsyn's exposure of Soviet concentration camps for nonconformists did not make communist repression any more popular a subject among artists in general or playwrights in particular.

The second crucial distinction between Stoppard and the "hairy men" is that his dramas are justly called comedies. Stoppard's dramaturgy, moreover, is often highly theatrical (sometimes in very conventional ways) and is often devoid of the naturalistic inclinations that usually accompany politically or socially committed playwrighting. Even if Stoppard's work up to 1975 is seen as an apprenticeship, a period of struggling to choose serious themes over spectacular effects, he has always contrived to bring about what he calls "the perfect marriage between the play of ideas and farce or perhaps even high comedy" ("Ambushes," p. 7). *Dirty Linen* and *New-Found-Land* is an exception to this, but in these plays Stoppard has readily identifiable and easily defined ideas on which he has made himself expert. Communist repression and journalism are matters with which he has had personal experience, having been born in Czechoslovakia and having worked as a reporter in Bristol.

Professional Foul was Stoppard's first work for television since *The Engagement* (1970), an elaboration of the plot and characters of *The Dissolution of Dominic Boot,* a 1964 radio play (see Hayman, pp. 24–25, 81–82). More importantly, *Professional Foul* stands structurally as well as thematically midway between *Jumpers* and *Every Good Boy Deserves Favor.* With *Jumpers,* it shares characters who are by occupation university professors of philosophy and whose cloistered and detached consideration of ethical problems is challenged by the events that surround them. *Every Good Boy Deserves Favor* shares with *Jumpers* the concern for free speech and thought in communist countries.

The play's title, a reference to a deliberate violation in sports, metaphorically suggests the behavior of its four philosophers: three Englishmen, Chetwyn, Anderson, and McKendrick, and an American, Stone. Stone, whose pursuits are openly mocked, is a linguistic philosopher whose epistomological observations verge on the tautological. Among the various avenues of philosophical inquiry discussed, his is the most rarefied and the least related to the political problems. Indeed, throughout the play Stone remains oblivious to the repressive nature of the Czech society that impinges on the lives of all three Englishmen. His subject is what Anderson and McKendrick can dismiss simply as a linguistic quirk: Through misunderstanding, language's inherent ambiguity, or the oddities of idiomatic expression, old can be young and young, old. Ironically, these possibilities for language form the basis of Stoppard's greatest acclaim as a manipulator of language and wit. McKendrick's final line in the first scene, for instance, is another illustration of the ambiguities inherent in language. When he asks himself, "I wonder if there'll be any decent women,"[4] he means not moral or respectable women, but just the opposite. Stone's address to the philosophical colloquium being held in Prague begins with the statement: "In a logical language there can be no ambiguity" (p. 71) and concludes: "And here I think the logical language, which can only be unambiguous, breaks down" (p. 74). All he has proven is that his initial premise was incorrect. Stone is the only one of the four philosophers to place such value on his work that he pursues his paltry observations at dinner; moreover, he demonstrates remarkably bad etiquette.

The three Englishmen (Anderson, Chetwyn, and McKendrick), on the other hand, are clearly distinguishable from one another on the basis of their extracurricular interests in attending the colloquium. Anderson, "the J. S. Mill Professor of Ethics at the University of Cambridge" (p. 78), is in Prague to see a qualifying match between England and Czechoslovakia for the World's Cup of soccer. Chetwyn, described by Anderson as "an ethics chap" and by McKendrick as believing "that Aristotle got it more or less right, and St. Augustine brought it up to date" (p. 47), is highly conscious of the political situation; he has, in fact, written letters to the London *Sunday Times* protesting the persecution of Czech academics. Finally, McKendrick, whose "field is the philosophical assumptions of social science" (p. 49), identifies himself as a Marxist but through most of the play pays little attention to the social or political situation in Czechoslovakia. Instead, he directs his energies toward reviewing jazz recordings for girly magazines, locating easy women in Prague, getting drunk, and insulting everyone within earshot.

On the flight from London to Prague, Anderson and McKendrick raise the basic philosophical question of *Professional Foul*:

4. Stoppard, *Professional Foul* in *Every Good Boy Deserves Favor and Professional Foul* (New York: Grove, 1978), p. 51.

ANDERSON:	Yes. To tell you the truth I have an ulterior motive for coming to Czechoslovakia at this time. I'm being a tiny bit naughty.
MCKENDRICK:	Naughty?
ANDERSON:	Unethical... Well, I am being paid for by the Czech government, after all.
MCKENDRICK:	And what...?
ANDERSON:	I don't think I'm going to tell you. You see, if I tell you, I make you a co-conspirator whether or not you would have wished to be one. Ethically I should not give you the opportunity of choosing to be or not.

(p. 48)

At this point in the play, Anderson is thinking only of his plans to escape the colloquium to attend a soccer game; he is not yet aware that his statement will come back to him with real import in the final scene. The distinction between naughty and unethical behavior, which is the crux of *Professional Foul*, will become increasingly apparent as the play unfolds.

Once Anderson arrives at his hotel in Prague, he is squarely confronted with an ethical dilemma that he would like to dismiss. Unfortunately for him, the more he attempts to exclude himself from the problems of a former student, Pavel Hollar, the more deeply he becomes involved. Hollar's doctoral thesis addresses the very questions Anderson prefers to ignore:

> The ethics of the State must be judged against the fundamental ethics of the individual. The human being, not the citizen. I [Hollar] conclude there is an obligation, a human responsibility, to fight against State correctness. Unfortunately that is not a safe conclusion.

(p. 61)

Anderson misunderstands Hollar, but the conclusion is unsafe on at least two counts: philosophically, the point is clearly debatable; politically, the conclusion challenges the Czech government's policy on the relationship between the state and the individual.

Anderson's first response to Hollar's request to smuggle the manuscript out of the country is refusal; since he is a guest of the Czech government, he argues "it would be bad manners, wouldn't it?" (p. 60). But bad manners are what Stone shows in talking with his mouth full of food at the dinner table. *Professional Foul* indicates a clear distinction between bad manners (speaking with one's mouth full of food) and bad morals (ignoring political oppression). The irony here is compounded by the fact that as linguists and philosophers these men can confuse manners and morals; their discipline should lead them to precision rather than slovenliness in using language.

Slowly, and by a process that necessarily entails some sacrifice on his part, Anderson accepts the responsibility, at least in an indirect fashion. First, however, he misses the soccer game that he had planned as his bit of naughtiness while the guest of the Czech government. When he attempts to return Hollar's manuscript the next day, he finds himself Mrs. Hollar's witness to the ransacking of her home by the Czech police who show little deference toward Anderson. Later, Anderson must confront Sacha, Hollar's son, who asks that Anderson return the manuscript but while Anderson deals with the ten-year-old boy as an adult and assures him that the efforts to obtain his father's release will be continued in England, Sacha breaks down and cries. The reality of Hollar's unjust imprisonment, the plight his family will surely endure in his absence, the menial labor he is assigned, finally goad Anderson into commitment.

Borrowing a typewriter from a British sports reporter covering the disastrous rout of the English soccer squad, Anderson writes an entirely new paper for presentation at the colloquium, a paper based on Hollar's thesis on "the conflict between the rights of the individuals and the rights of the community" (p. 111). The Czech chairman of Anderson's session realizes that he cannot allow such a paper to be presented. He first attempts to silence Anderson by explaining that the translators cannot work without a prepared text and, when that fails, by sounding the fire alarm and evacuating the meeting room.

Almost as if he had anticipated the chairman's ploy, Anderson has planted Hollar's manuscript in McKendrick's luggage. At customs, Anderson and Chetwyn are thoroughly searched by the authorities, while McKendrick breezes through the inspection. Anderson, of course, clears the authorities, but Chetwyn is found to be carrying documents that incriminate not only himself but also the Czech whose letters to Amnesty International and the United Nations he was trying to smuggle out of the country. The play comes full circle in returning to the ethical question that was raised in the first meeting of Anderson and McKendrick. Anderson argues that Chetwyn should have known that the Czech authorities were suspicious of him and would search him before allowing him to leave. McKendrick, the Marxist supposedly interested in social and political questions, states flatly that he would not have undertaken such a task only to learn that he has already accomplished it. Anderson admits that he "reversed a principle" (p. 124) but argues that the point was that McKendrick would not be searched whereas he, in all likelihood, would be.

Professional Foul recalls *Jumpers* not only in its use of philosophers but also in its enactment of abstract beliefs. McKendrick, like George, professes a philosophy that should direct him to full engagement in political and social realities; but as for Moore his actions belie his beliefs. Anderson, like McFee, moves from intellectual detachment to political commitment. Moreover, the three English philosophers also recall the three English artists in *Artist Descending a Staircase.* Each represents a different view and practice of art or philosophy; although these six characters cannot be paired off in corresponding sets, each must venture outside the comfort and seclusion of his discipline to face reality.

Thematically, *Professional Foul* is most closely related to *Every Good Boy Deserves Favor.* The preface to Stoppard's collaboration with André Previn provides a record of this play's evolution. The preface, ironically entitled "Nothing in Mind," records that when, in 1974, Previn first approached him with the project, Stoppard thought that since an orchestra would appear on stage, its presence could be justified if it were owned by a millionaire. Later, he realized it could be "a mere delusion of the millionaire's brain. Once the orchestra became an imaginary orchestra, there was no need for the millionaire to be a millionaire either. I changed tack: the play would be about a lunatic triangle-player who thought he had an orchestra."[5] Months later, in April 1976, Stoppard met Victor Fainberg, a Russian dissident who had been imprisoned in mental hospitals for his political protest of the Soviet invasion of Czechoslovakia. Fainberg would serve as an inspiration for the character of Alexander; the other essential characters—the lunatic triangle-player, the dissident's son—were then drawn as principal figures for the play. But that *Every Good Boy Deserves Favor* developed as a clear political statement against the Soviet persecution of political and artistic dissidents is not nearly as accidental as Stoppard's preface might suggest. Albert E. Kalson notes that at the same time,

> Mrs. Previn, Mia Farrow, was appearing with the Royal Shakespeare Company together with John Wood— Stoppard's favorite actor, for whom he wrote *Travesties*—in a 1976 production of Chekhov's *Ivanov*. The result is a serious comic play in which Wood once again plays a confused Russian named Ivanov, and Previn indulges his considerable talent for musical parody and pastiche with Prokofiev his unmistakable source.
>
> (p. 562)

By 1976, Stoppard's interest in the political situation in his native Czechoslovakia had been clearly aroused. In February of the next year, he had written an article for *The New York Times*, "Dirty Linen in Prague," which had nothing whatsoever to do with his plays but dealt exclusively with political repression of Czech artists and intellectuals and which paid particular attention to the imprisonment of Vaclav Havel, a Czech playwright. Stoppard's essay meticulously details the response of the Western press, particularly in Britain, to the issuance of Charter 77, a document that reiterated the conditions and privileges supposedly assured by the 1975 Helsinki Agreement. Stoppard leaves no doubt as to his own position in his conclusion:

5. Stoppard, "Nothing in Mind," programme for the production of *Every Good Boy Deserves Favor* at the Mermaid Theatre, 1978.

For Havel's sake and a great deal more, isn't it really time we told them that a human right is not an "internal affair," that signing a petition is not a "serious crime" against any state which claims to be civilized, that a weasel is not a bloody whale? And went on telling them at the highest level?[6]

Meanwhile, in December 1976, Fainberg's efforts secured the release of Vladimir Bukovsky, "the off-stage hero of *Every Good Boy Deserves Favor* referred to as 'my friend C.'" Six months later, Stoppard met Bukovsky in London and invited him to attend a rehearsal of the play that opened on 1 July 1977.

The central metaphor in *Every Good Boy Deserves Favor* is that of "an insistent, discordant note, one might say, in an orchestrated society." Most obviously, the note is struck by Alexander, the prisoner who, according to his doctors, imagines that the Soviet government would imprison political dissidents in mental institutions. But that same note reverberates throughout the play: Alexander's son, Sacha, plays what is described as a "subversive triangle" (p. 14); Alexander's cell-mate, Ivanov, imagines that he conducts an orchestra. Each of them fails to conform to the score that the state has designated for them to play; each relies upon his own apprehension of the world—of its injustices, music, and reality. Not coincidentally, all three of these characters are named Alexander Ivanov, which, in the sleight-of-hand conclusion to the play is the only thing that saves them from the Soviet system.

The ethical question raised by Alexander's capitulation is: Can he compromise his conscience to admit publicly that his imprisonment did, in fact, not exist? As in Brecht's *Galileo*, the protagonist is ordered to capitulate; with his recantation will come release from physical torment but the onset of intellectual anguish because the capitulation will fuel the machinery of repression. Sacha directly challenges his father on this point:

6. Stoppard, "Dirty Linen in Prague," *The New York Times* (11 February 1977), p. 27.

SACHA: Tell them lies. Tell them they've cured you. Tell them you're grateful.
ALEX: How can that be right?
SACHA: If they're wicked how can it be wrong?
ALEX: It helps them to go on being wicked. It helps people to think that perhaps they're not so wicked after all.

(p. 36)

Sacha's argument is perhaps best summarized by his statement that it is wicked if Alexander allows himself to die by refusing to capitulate or by continuing his hunger strike. Alexander, however, asserts his own courage and believes, finally, that he has defeated the authorities:

Then I went on a hunger strike. And when they saw I intended to die they lost their nerve. And now you think I'm going to crawl out of here, thanking them for curing me of my delusions? Oh no. They lost. And they will have to see that it is so. They have forgotten their mortality. Losing might be their first touch of it for a long time.

(p. 28)

There is, undoubtedly, an idealism here that is rare in Stoppard's work, but it is counterbalanced by the savagery of Alexander's own comments on his life. Speaking with a forthrightness intensified by the purity of his convictions, Alexander demonstrates that at least the hope of individual victory over repression and degradation still exists. His is the affirmation of human dignity and freedom against impossible odds.

The ending of *Every Good Boy Deserves Favor* recalls Sacha's refrain, "Every thing can be all right" (p. 39, passim), for only through the ineptitude of Colonel Rozinsky, or perhaps his enthusiasm to produce a high rate of successful "cures," is Alexander released. Colonel Rozinsky, ironically a Doctor of Philology who specializes in semantics and thereby parallels the boorish Stone of *Professional Foul*, confuses the two Alexander Ivanovs. Hence, he releases both a political dissident who is willing to admit that he does not hear an orchestra and a madman who acknowledges that the state does not put sane men in insane asylums for their political beliefs.

Night and Day was Stoppard's first commercial success designed for the West End audience to incorporate the political inclination of *Professional Foul* and *Every Good Boy Deserves Favor*. *Night and Day* opened at the Phoenix Theatre in London on 8 November 1978, a production starring Diana Rigg and directed by Peter Wood. Initially, the critics responded favorably but seemed to dwell on the differences between this play and Stoppard's earlier work. Harold Hobson, writing for *Drama*, was typical in his observation that *Night and Day* "departs from his usual manner . . . in contrast with Stoppard's previous work, it is a comparatively straightforward play."[7] The Faber paperback edition of the play identifies it as "a change of direction from the literary high jinks of *Jumpers* and *Travesties*."

While clearly well in line with the recent developments in his works since the time of *Jumpers*, *Night and Day* demonstrates remarkable similarities with previous plays as well as significant differences. Even the most important departures from the style of his previous plays might have been expected in light of *Professional Foul* and *Every Good Boy Deserves Favor*.

The plot indicates few similarities with the farcical style that characterizes even the works which immediately precede *Night and Day*. Set in a mythical but politically typical African country in the late seventies, *Night and Day* presents an international political situation—not unlike the victory of the Radical Liberals in *Jumpers* or in World War I in *Travesties*—which frames the action of the characters. The connection between this political situation and the lives of the play's characters is especially important here because several of them are reporters sent to Kambawe to cover the civil strife. The dispute is all too familiar to political observers of African affairs: a group of rebels, ostensibly controlled by one Colonel Shimbu and backed by communist supplies, pilots, and technical assistance, initiates a civil war against the established regime. In this particular instance, the present powers derive from the military victory of a nationalistic military organization that wrenched political power from the British. Moreover, a

7. Harold Hobson, "Plays in Performance," review of *Night and Day*, *Drama* 131 (Winter 1979): 42.

victory by the communist-supported group that seeks to break away from President Mageeba's government would also mean an end to the mining operation of Geoffrey Carson's company.

The linchpin of the subplots of *Night and Day* is Ruth Carson's one-night stand with a reporter, Richard Wagner. Although Ruth offers a plausible explanation for her moment of weakness ("I let you take me to dinner because there was no danger of going to bed with you. And then, because there was no danger of going to bed a second time, I went to bed with you." [p. 54]), the affair is regrettably contrived. Unlike most of his previous works, the characters in *Night and Day* tread more realistic ground. Gone are the fantastic coincidences that underlie *Travesties*, the bizarre machinations of *Jumpers*, and the anachronistic and impossible action of *Rosencrantz and Guildenstern*. But in their place stands Ruth's prosaic and unpleasant affair with Wagner.

The other dramaturgical device that links *Night and Day* with the earlier plays are the two voices of Ruth. The dramatically vivid (but thoroughly confusing) imagination of Ruth governs the beginning of Act 2. Stoppard's note on "Ruth" offers this explanation:

> The audience is occasionally made privy to RUTH's thought, and to hers alone. This text makes no reference to the technique by which this is achieved. (It may be that—ideally—no technical indication is necessary.) When RUTH's thoughts are audible she is simply called "RUTH" in quotes, and treated as a separate character. Thus, RUTH can be interrupted by "RUTH."
>
> (p. 13)

In the original London production with Diana Rigg, no technical device was necessary; the distinction was made instead mainly by turning a full eye to the audience. Since many of "Ruth's" early comments are song lyrics (from Cole Porter's "Night and Day" and Lennon's and McCartney's "Help!") there was no difficulty in highlighting those transitions. In essence, they are asides to the audience complicated by "Ruth's" capacity for self-detachment and self-criticism and the ability to incorporate other characters in the dramatic action of those asides. "Ruth's" asides are analogous to George Moore's composition of his symposium lecture while addressing an imaginary mirror in the fourth wall; to Gladys's (of *If You're Glad, I'll Be Frank*) rhapsodic interior monologues; and to Albert's lofty, sardonic observations.

But "Ruth" in *Night and Day* most closely resembles Old Carr in *Travesties*. Just as the erratic memory of Old Carr governed what was enacted on stage, so too at the beginning of Act 2, the lively imagination of "Ruth" shows us fantasy rather than reality. The entire sequence between Milne and Ruth that opens the second act takes place not in fact but in Ruth's mind. By the play's end, the audience realizes that the scene is impossible because it opens with Milne's return from Shimbu's camp; Milne, of course, never returns because he is killed there. Like some of the scenes from *Travesties*, this encounter is played twice because it is controlled by "Ruth's" imagination, and she realizes her first effort turns bad. The impossibility of the scene is made clear by Stoppard's stage directions:

> MILNE turns and walks up-stage into the dark and disappears. RUTH's feet disappear out of sight behind the sofa and then "she" (double) stands up with her back to the audience looking toward where MILNE disappeared, undoes her dress and steps out of it (she has nothing on underneath) holding on to the dress with one hand and trailing it after her as she follows MILNE into the dark. Before she has disappeared CARSON has walked unhurriedly, relaxed, into the room from the side of the stage. He lights a cigarette and stands thoughtfully watching as RUTH moves into the dark. (After a moment or two, behind him, RUTH's voice:
> RUTH: Got a cigarette? (She is lying on the sofa behind CARSON.)
>
> (p. 70)

Just as Old Carr's memory controlled the events depicted in *Travesties* and Albert's favorable perception of life depended on his distance from others in *Albert's Bridge*, the importance of perspective is realistically epitomized in journalism. Not only can journalists manipulate opinion in writing a story, but even in presenting it. As incentive to Mageeba, Wagner holds out the promise that an exclusive interview would receive very favorable treatment in the *Globe*:

MAGEEBA: That's very fair. Isn't it Geoffrey? Mr. Wagner says I can have equal space.

WAGNER: And some space is more equal than others. I think, sir, I could more or less guarantee that an interview with you at this juncture of the war would be treated as the main news story of the day, and of course would be picked up by the newspapers, and all the media, round the world.

MAGEEBA: What war, Mr. Wagner?

(p. 78)

The newspapers, then, not only manipulate opinion, but events; they can transform a separatist movement into a war. The power of the press is not restricted to the reporting of facts and informing the public, but also extends to the fabrication of reality. By labeling a war as such, reporting creates its own self-fulfilling prophecies.

Wagner's tactics in both love and war are thoroughly Machiavellian. He tacitly assumes that because his trade is sanctioned as the cornerstone of democracy, he can use whatever means he chooses. Wagner strongly believes that the strength and freedom of journalists depend upon their trade union; without the union, they would have no safeguard against capitalistic owners and capricious management. Chagrined over Milne's exclusive interview (which is the result of luck, individual incentive, and his willingness to take risks), Wagner files a protest with Battersby, the union representative, because the *Globe* printed a story by Milne who does not belong to the union. Wagner's arguments for a closed shop are probably less sympathetic than even Mageeba's support for a "relatively free press" (a free press edited by one of his relatives [p. 85]). Not only is Wagner an unattractive person who exploits his host, deceives his colleagues, and taunts his hostess, but he also instigates the strike that shuts down the *Globe* rendering his and Guthrie's efforts and Milne's death meaningless. Wagner, in fact, demands that the union prevent the *Globe* from printing Milne's stories, the closest thing to news that reaches print in the course of the play.

100

The central disagreement between Wagner and Magee-ba is the "lobby system"—that journalistic practice of offering prime and extensive coverage of a given position in return for interviews and exclusive information. Wagner so values his own powers as a reporter that he thinks the promise of "lobby basis" (p. 72) coverage will be sufficient to assuage Mageeba's anger and Carson's embarrassment at having a British reporter present at a delicate and crucial moment in negotiations for the future of Kambawe.

However vague or ill-defined Ruth's feelings about journalism were in Act 1, Milne's death brings her to the conviction that he died not for any noble principle but only for the lamentable state of British reportage:

> And the winner isn't democracy, it's just business. As far as I'm concerned, Jake died for the product. He died for the women's page, and the crossword, and the racing results, and the heartbreak beauty queen and somewhere at the end of a long list I suppose he died for the leading article too, but it's never worth *that*—
>
> (p. 91)

Ruth's analysis is not grounded simply in remorse or regret; instead, she appreciates the paradox of a free press: only without governmental constraints is the press truly free to publish the truth, but then it must rely upon a readership that will financially support the expense of ascertaining the truth. Unlike Lenin, she realizes that intellectual freedom sometimes entails unpleasant and even reprehensible practices.

Ultimately, *Night and Day* can be seen as an ironic attack against the entire journalistic system—against the unions that can deprive the public of the news through labor actions; against the journalists themselves who squander whatever real talents they have to produce titillating copy; against the reading public that supports and rewards those same misdirected efforts. These are, however, the conclusions to which the audience is merely led; they are not voiced by a single character whose opinion is transparently more credible than all the others. But these particular conclusions appear to be the only ones supported by the play itself.

Stoppard's most recent work, *Dogg's Hamlet, Cahoot's Macbeth* (1979), advances his concern with the communist repression of intellectual and artistic freedom, particularly in the latter playlet that is dedicated to the Czech playwright Pavel Kohout. Kohout provides a touchstone for considering not only Stoppard's most recent work but also *Rosencrantz and Guildenstern*. The lives and careers of Kohout and Stoppard are, in fact, linked by a network of coincidence so bizarre as to have possibly come from one of Stoppard's own plays. Not only were Stoppard and Kohout both born in Czechoslovakia, but both have adapted Shakespearean tragedy for performance by noncommercial, community-oriented groups; both have written plays that rely upon audience familiarity with the themes, characters, and plot of *Hamlet*.

Although Stoppard's plays are well known to American and Western European audiences, Kohout's are not. *Poor Murderer* (1971) is his only play produced on Broadway or in the West End; Kohout himself has never seen it performed. Indeed, he has at least seventeen additional plays and dramatic adaptations completed. All of them, including *Poor Murderer*, are banned from production in Czechoslovakia.

A former party member, Kohout and other liberal compatriots were purged from prominence when the Soviets stormed Prague. The censorship of his (and numerous others') works attracted international attention in early 1977 with the publication of Charter 77, a document enumerating the freedoms theoretically guaranteed by the Helsinki Agreement but systematically denied the Czechs. Among those who investigated and wrote about the harassment of Kohout and other prominent Czech authors (as well as other intellectuals, workers, and artists) was Stoppard whose essays on the suppression in Czechoslovakia appeared in *The New York Review of Books* and *The New York Times*.[8]

These essays and Stoppard's "Preface" to *Cahoot's Macbeth* make explicit the political views that informed *Professional Foul* and *Every Good Boy Deserves Favor*:

---

8. Stoppard, "Prague: The Story of the Chartists," *The New York Review of Books* (4 August 1977), pp. 11–15.

During the last decade of "normalization" which followed the fall of Dubcek [sic], thousands of Czechoslovaks have been prevented from pursuing their careers. Among them are many writers and actors.

During a short visit to Prague in 1977 I met Kohout and Pavel Landovsky, a well known actor who had been banned from working for years, since falling foul of the authorities.[9]

This meeting led to correspondence between Kohout and Stoppard that brought to light their apparently coincidental adaptations of Shakespeare for community theatre groups. In 1976, Stoppard's "(The 15 Minute) Dogg's Troup Hamlet" was first performed by one of the four experimental companies that comprise Inter-Action. *Dogg's Hamlet* draws upon that 1976 adaptation and adds a prefatory episode in which the stage is prepared for *Hamlet* by a trio of schoolboys whose native language is Dogg. (Dogg is a language that uses English words but with entirely different lexical meanings. When, for instance, a dignified matron offers a ceremonial greeting in Dogg, she says: "Scabs, slobs, black yobs, yids, spicks, wops . . . [As one might say 'Your grace, ladies and gentlemen, boys and girls']"). Kohout's analogous adaptation of Shakespeare, growing out of vastly different circumstances, is reported by Stoppard in the "Preface":

A year later [1978] Kohout wrote to me: "As you know, many Czech theatre-people are not allowed to work in the theatre during the last years. As one of them who cannot live without theatre, I was searching for a possibility to do theatre in spite of circumstances. Now I am glad to tell you that in a few days, after eight weeks of rehearsal—a Living-Room Theatre is opening, with nothing smaller but Macbeth."

Cahoot's Macbeth is Stoppard's imaginary dramatization of the arbitrary harassment the Czech authorities inflict on this adaptation of *Macbeth*. As Stoppard notes, "However, Cahoot is not Kohout, and this necessarily over-truncated Macbeth is not supposed to be a fair representation of Kohout's elegant seventy-five minute version."

9. Stoppard, *Dogg's Hamlet/Cahoot's Macbeth* (London: Inter-Action Imprint, N.D.), N.P.

103

Cahoot's Macbeth, written for the British American Repertory Company and presented by Inter-Action, begins with the condensation of *Macbeth* to Act 3, Scene 2, into six pages of dialogue. At that point, in response to incessant rapping at the door (which parallels the Porter scene in Shakespeare's play), an Inspector from the state police enters with the line: "Oh—I'm sorry—is this the National Theatre?" Ironically, his statement reminds the audience of the repression of theatrical freedom in communist countries.

The potentially menacing police detective has been a recurrent character in Stoppard's work from the time of Inspector Hound in *The Real Inspector Hound* (1968) through Inspector Foot in *After Magritte* (1970) to Inspector Bones in *Jumpers* (1972). These detectives were, however, benignly incompetent rather than malevolent. With the Inspector of *Cahoot's Macbeth*, the sadistic impulses and sinister wit (with which Joe Orton endowed his Inspector Truscott of *Loot*) become the character's distinguishing attributes. Indeed, Stoppard's Inspector, like Truscott, has a stinging rejoinder for virtually every sentence uttered by his victims:

> INSPECTOR: (to LADY MACBETH). Darling, you were marvellous.
> "LADY": I'm not your darling.
> INSPECTOR: I know, and you weren't marvellous either, but when in Rome parlevous as the natives do. Actually, I thought you were better on the radio.
> "LADY": I haven't been on the radio.
> INSPECTOR: You've been on mine.

The Inspector's prey avoided arrest only through the accidental and illogical appearance of one of the schoolboys from *Dogg's Hamlet*. Sharing a phrase book of the Dogg language with the actors, the schoolboy enables them to complete their performance of *Macbeth* in Dogg, a feat that both befuddles and frustrates the Inspector.

Politically, *Cahoot's Macbeth* ends only with "a theatrical finale" rather than true resolution. Like *Every Good Boy Deserves Favor*, which climaxes when the prisoner accused of political dissidence is freed only because he is confused with a mentally disturbed patient, *Cahoot's Macbeth* ends not with political commitment but with comic legerdemain. Stoppard's political comment, however, is unmistakably lucid: artistic repression is rampant in his native country. That he chooses to convey this in a comic rather than didactic play should diminish neither the urgency of his cause nor the sincerity of his concern.

The canon of Stoppard's work up to 1980 shares much with post-World War II art and literature in general and with contemporary British drama in particular. His works invite comparisons with the visual arts both because of his consideration of aesthetic questions through the eyes of painters (as in *Artist* or *Travesties*) or because of his extensive and often elaborate references to artists (as in *After Magritte*). His mutual concern with these artists is the nature, function, and responsibility of art. Underlying these perennial issues is a self-consciousness characteristic of contemporary art and literature. The most obvious examples of this self-consciousness are the painters of the postwar period who explore the specific limits and nature of their media. The works of Rothko, Pollock, Reinhardt, and others implicitly ask: What is a painting? Must it express or represent an object or an emotion? Must it have certain tangible features (color, form, texture, content)? Must it physically exist at all? In drama, the absurdists approach such questions at least implicitly by omitting elements formerly judged indispensable to drama—elements such as consistent characterization, unified plot, logical development, and conflict. While Stoppard never rarefies the questions he asks of art to the extreme of the abstract expressionists or of the absurdist playwrights, he does deal with the problem of the nature of his medium and, more specifically, the responsibilities of the artist in society. Stoppard's self-scrutiny also evokes the work of the metafictionists, notably Coover, Barth, and Fowles. The important distinction between them and Stoppard, however, is that Stoppard deliberately and selflessly distances himself from his work. He never indulges in the narcissism of the autobiographical impulse in his characterizations. The closest his characters come to his own life are the drama critics of *The Real Inspector Hound* and the journalists of *Night and Day*. But at least when exploring the processes and methods of creative artists, he has drawn characters who usually do not work in the medium of language. In turn, this self-consciousness has engendered a virtual obsession with the question of perspective. Characters, especially protagonists, are often afforded a means of voicing their personal thought directly to the audience. Old Carr's erratic memory, "Ruth's" imaginary interludes in *Night and Day*, Gladys's and Albert's rhapsodic monologues, and George's lecture are all examples of the personal voice that grows out of Stoppard's concern with perspective.

But Stoppard's brand of "distance" from his characters is antithetical to the celebrated "distancing" of Bertolt Brecht's *Verfremsdungeffect* as well as the autobiographical or confessional impulse that fuels the metafictionists. Brecht's V-effect was primarily intended to distance the audience and, hence, instill in them a greater objectivity or critical awareness of the events on stage. Instead, Stoppard's technique, even in his most didactic plays, is for the playwright to distance himself. Rather than heavy-handedly weighting the arguments that the playwright himself espouses, Stoppard often makes those arguments ludicrous; if not, at least the counterarguments are given fair voice. By not idealizing those characters who best represent Stoppard's own opinions, he renders them no more credible than the others.

Second, and corollary to the concern with the nature of art, is Stoppard's consciousness of the dramatic tradition that nurtures him. This demands a thorough knowledge and profound understanding of the theatre, its techniques, and history. The most obvious example of the consciousness of the dramatic tradition in Stoppard's work is in his borrowing, some might say theft, from Wilde and Shakespeare. Moreover, it also accounts for Stoppard's penchant for and skill in parodying popular dramatic genres. Like most contemporary playwrights, he has not contented himself with the confines of representational drama but has broken out of those constraints by revivifying the soliloquy, aside, song, and interior monologue. Structurally, Stoppard manipulates the fourth wall of representational theatre by mining the traditions of drama to recover vehicles for direct address to the audience. This leads to the play-life metaphor that appears in *Rosencrantz and Guildenstern*, *The Real Inspector Hound*, and *Travesties*. Certainly, Stoppard's experience as a drama critic has substantially contributed to his keen awareness of the dramatic tradition.

Third, Stoppard's treatment of language allies him not only with the absurdists but also with the wittiest if not greatest writers of the English language. Like Conrad, Stoppard may have had the advantage of learning English as a second language and thus with a greater sensitivity to the ironies and nuances of its idiom. His use of puns, quid pro quo, and other forms of wordplay is perhaps his most acclaimed and best known characteristic. Like all brilliant comic writers who employ the English language, Stoppard indulges himself as well as his audience in the sheer pleasure of experiencing the density and richness of which the language is capable. Moreover, his attention to language results not only in humor but also in precision. As a means of considering the difficulty of communication as well as a comic vehicle, language is assiduously explored and exploited by Stoppard.

Fourth, Stoppard's work accommodates both an elitism and a community-oriented populism. His artistic and financial contributions to Inter-Action, most notably *Dirty Linen*, is indicative of his commitment to noncommercial theatre. The elitism of his work, which is often economic as well as intellectual, is inherent in his strong consciousness of the dramatic tradition and his highly theatrical style. Only the resources of a sophisticated commercial (or state-supported) theatre can effectively produce *Jumpers* or *Every Good Boy Deserves Favor*. Although these plays are unlikely undertakings for community and noncommercial threatre groups, others, like *Dogg's Hamlet* and *After Magritte*, were originally written for and remain accessible to such groups.

Although Stoppard's self-consciousness, concern for language, and sensitivity to dramatic tradition place him in the mainstream of contemporary drama, other features of his work mark him as something of a reactionary. To some critics, his theatricalism suggests an atavistic return to nineteenth-century farce; others regard his cleverness as a ruse to disguise his lack of profundity. Stoppard's insistence upon comedy as his métier, even when dealing with serious issues, has provoked many commentators. During the 1960s and 1970s, when great drama was generally identified with the solemnity, gravity, and even pretentiousness of other playwrights, Stoppard's work allies him with the masters of the comic tradition. Like the best comic dramatists, his gift for language and physical comedy fuses with an acute perception of the excesses, eccentricities, and foibles of man. If his plays endure, Stoppard's unique accomplishment may prove to be the theatrical treatment of the intellectual and artistic follies of our age.

Considered along a political spectrum, Stoppard's plays tend toward the right. This century has had flocks of leftist playwrights, but Stoppard, while hardly embracing the status quo in the manner of escapist authors, addresses political issues from a conservative vantage. The history of drama, especially in the twentieth century, suggests that comedy and political commitment have little common ground. But Stoppard's faith in man and his characters' persistent, if battered, optimism are aptly suited to his comic mode.

Stoppard's preoccupation with language is not only the mainstay of his acclaim as a wit but also a serious thematic interest that can be traced throughout his work. His canon to date is fashioned of a consistent texture of characters, motifs, and themes. His recurrent character type, despite frequent unhappy ends, demands comic presentation because of the character's spirited faith in himself. Most of his protagonists weather disappointment, disaster, and even doom without despair. Their circumstances are often comfortable, but their lives are never easy.

Stoppard's plays, like their settings and their characters' games, are self-contained systems invariably predicated on and dedicated to logic. The plays hardly inspire audiences to action outside the theatre; yet they illustrate the choices—political, philosophical, and ethical—that confront contemporary man. Like games, the plays often have their own internal logic that can transport the audience from the world of missed connections to a tidily wrapped microcosm.

Stoppard's accomplishment as a craftsman of plot is not to be underestimated. Although audiences and critics have sometimes been frustrated by the tangents the plays pursue, his works withstand textual analysis and perhaps even fare better for it. In writing specifically for performance, for what will work best on stage, he also has created plays that grow richer with careful scrutiny.